"When I was young I was sure of everything; in a few years, having been mistaken a thousand times, I was not half so sure of most things as I was before; at present, I am hardly sure of anything but what God has revealed to me."

John Wesley

UNDERSTANDING

Jesus

in the 21st Century

To Bishop Karen, with great gratitude.

[illegible]

Dr. Michael D. Dent

Foreword by Rev. John Danforth
Former United States Senator

Understanding Jesus in the 21st Century

books@marketsquarebooks.com
P.O. Box 23664 Knoxville, Tennessee 37933

ISBN: 978-1-950899-19-7
Library of Congress: 2021931131

Printed and Bound in the United States of America

Publisher: Kevin Slimp
Editor: Kristin Lighter
Post-Process Editor: Ken Rochelle

Table of Contents

Foreword 1
The Honorable John C. Danforth

Preface 5

Introduction 9

Chapter One 13
Jesus and Racism

Chapter Two 21
Jesus and Politics: I have a Candidate

Chapter Three 29
Jesus and Politics: How Faithful People Can Change Politics

Chapter Four 37
Looking for Transformational Leaders

Chapter Five 45
Jesus and the Jews: What About Our Jewish Friends?

Chapter Six 53
Jesus and Other Religions: One Way or Many?

Chapter Seven 63
Jesus and Human Sexuality: Bringing the "L Word" Home

Chapter Eight 77
Jesus the Refugee

Chapter Nine 85
Jesus and the Most Interesting Man in the World

Chapter Ten 93
Jesus and Football

Chapter Eleven 101
Jesus and Christopher Columbus

Chapter Twelve 107
Jesus and Willie Nelson

Chapter Thirteen 115
Jesus and Osama bin Laden

Chapter Fourteen 121
Jesus and Contentment

Chapter Fifteen 129
Jesus in a Pandemic World

Chapter Sixteen 137
Jesus and 4-G Thanksgiving

Chapter Seventeen 143
Jesus and Pets

Chapter Eighteen 153
Jesus and My Life Purpose

Foreword

The Honorable John C. Danforth

We live in the post-Protestant era, a time statistically measured by the collapse of mainline churches. Over the last two decades, church membership has declined by 16.9 percent. Some causes are beyond our control as Sundays have emerged from the old blue laws and become times for sports, shopping, and sleeping in. It is hard for churches to compete with Sunday morning soccer games. But most of the decline is our own fault as we have ceased providing much that is not readily available in the secular realm.

We offer bromides for happy lives, but so does Dr. Phil. We offer opinions on public issues, but so do political parties. It is quite reasonable for many to conclude that the churches have nothing special to add to what we already know, so why bother with church?

Commitment to social causes is within a strong Biblical tradition extending from the prophets of ancient Israel to the admonition by Jesus that we must care for the "least of these" among us. But we need not be Christians to commit ourselves to the same causes; indeed, we might be agnostic or atheists and be what many would call "good people." Where we have failed has been in spelling out what it means to be not only a good person but a Christian person. We have given the appearance of being just like any other good people; good, but not specifically religious. Author Joseph Bottum has described mainline Protestantism as "a social gospel without the gospel," and has called my denomination, the Episcopal Church, "the National Organization for Women at Prayer."

Michael Dent's *Understanding Jesus in the 21st Century* is rich with wisdom tales for the living of these days. It is contemporary, speaking to the modern reader's personal and social life. On the personal level, it addresses the concerns of all of us: What is the meaning of life? How do we face death? How do we approach marriage, divorce, raising a family? On the social level, Dent unflinchingly raises today's controversial issues: gay marriage, immigration reform, how to fix our broken politics.

What sets Michael Dent apart from the "social gospel without the gospel" is that all of his commentary is connected directly to the Christian faith. It is not the case that his message could be delivered by any good person, even a well-meaning non-believer. What he says is specifically religious. In other words, if we are not the ones to deliver our message, nobody will. Here are some of his key points that set us apart from other "good people."

We believe in one God, and that belief puts every other interest in context. Dent cites the great 20th Century theologian Paul Tillich's definition of religious faith as the expression of "ultimate concern." All of us have numerous concerns, wealth, success, and status among them, but only one concern can be ultimate, and that is God.

When we permit anything else to take first place in our lives, we lose perspective. We resemble caricatures drawn by cartoonists with one aspect drawn grotesquely out of proportion.

As Dent explains it, "We will never enjoy the abundant, joyful, and fulfilling life as long as we are at the center of our lives." This is a message about how to live a fulfilling life, but it is not what we can find in any self-improvement book or advice column. It is specifically and uniquely based on religious faith.

We are called to live not only for ourselves but for others. The model here is the self-giving love of Christ on the Cross, and it is the opposite of any advice we may receive about how to get ahead in life. Indeed, the counter intuitive message of Christianity is that the way to gain your life is to lose it. Dent frames this as hospitality to strangers and concern for "the hurting, the hungry, the homeless," all cases where from any worldly point of view the giver has something to lose and nothing to gain. Religion specifically calls on us to be losers. No one else does. It is our message, and ours alone.

Religion calls us into communion with others, an especially important message at a time when we have turned in on ourselves. As this veteran pastor explains, "Religion is communal. It has the power to bring us together in a world where many are wearing headphones, or gazing at a screen, or texting, tweeting, or talking into a portable electronic device." This pattern of self-isolation has been going on for some time, and it has been exacerbated by the social distancing required by COVID-19 to the point where some have suggested that it has become the "new normal." We who are entrusted with the ministry of reconciliation and who believe that in Christ all things hold together cannot let it be the new normal. It must be our special ministry to bridge divisions. Again, if not us, who?

Michael Dent is a gifted pastor with a life of distinguished ministry in Texas and Colorado. Now, he is sharing his specifically religious insights with a broader audience.

Preface

Michael D. Dent

On June 28, 2017, my life changed forever in an unexpected and unwelcomed way. I was diagnosed with mild cognitive impairment. MCI is a neurological condition which affects one's short term memory. For months I had been experiencing some forgetfulness, repeating the same question in five minutes or less time, and misplacing my keys, pen, wallet, or cell phone. Naturally, I denied and dismissed the notion anything was wrong with me beyond normal aging deficits. After 64 years of never spending a night in the hospital as a patient, I was depressed and anxious with the diagnosis.

The young neurology expert at the University of Colorado Anschutz Medical Campus was professional, straightforward, and yet hopeful. Nonetheless, my life had taken a new turn toward an uncertain outcome. The best would be no further progression of the mild impairment. The worst scenario would be a rapid deterioration into full-blown Alzheimer's disease and eventually death. The reality of my diagnosis hit home hard when Sharon, my wife of 43 years, and I picked up the prescription at the pharmacy later that day. The label on the pill bottle had my name on it with this command:

> **Take one tablet by mouth for mild to moderate Alzheimer type dementia.**

Holy heck.

Three months later on my 65th birthday, Sharon stood with me at the center pulpit at Trinity Church at the close of each service. It was no happy birthday. We shared my diagnosis and our decision to retire June 30, 2018, a year earlier than planned. We shared more than a few tears that day after each service. We were most grateful for hugs, promises of prayer, cards, and notes.

Over the next eight months, I participated in several research testing and exams at the Anschutz Medical Campus. These voluntary procedures included a lumbar puncture, MRI, memory tests, ophthalmology exams, and exercises. In the MRI procedure, lying still for 70 minutes in a tube without moving or scratching my nose brought me remarkably close to the Divine. These procedures may not have helped me, but the research results may well benefit others who are diagnosed with cognitive impairments.

As it turned out, I had to retire in April 2018 due to my declining health condition. The good gift of retirement enabled me to begin my ministerial memoir sooner than expected. *Love Whispers: Reflections of a Seasoned Pastor* was published in December 2019. One seasoned reviewer has written:

> *What would you expect of a pastor's memoir? The author begins one chapter with these words: "Being a pastor means more than being able to marry, bury, and save Uncle Harry." The book, Love Whispers, peppered with wit, nostalgia, and humor, proves to be infinitely more than a peek into routine and provincial church life. Instead be ready for a ministry that intersects directly with national and international events, provides close proximity to heroes, celebrities, and superstars, and gives rise to outreaches of compassion to such arenas as Haiti and the AIDS crisis.*

The over-arching theme of the book is a welcome melody for our present society: that there are whispers of love in the midst of dark times. As the author shares his discernment of 'love whispers,' readers are invited to listen for their own. Dent concludes his book with a prayer for the reader's life and an eventual benediction to his own: "Love never ends. May its whispers and the Whisperer bless you on the journey ahead. There is no place love cannot whisper." Indeed.

Because of the of the nature of my health challenge and our lifelong commitment to generosity, Sharon and I decided to donate a tithe (10 percent) of the proceeds of that book to the Alzheimer's Association. Truth be told, we are giving far more than that. One in three senior adults dies with Alzheimer's or other dementia. Your family is likely to be touched by dementia if it has not already.

We have decided to give again to the Alzheimer's Association at least 10 percent of all purchases of *Understanding Jesus in the 21st Century.* Thank you for your investment in the effort to reduce Alzheimer's disease, which accounts for up to 80 percent of all dementia. A cure for the disease remains elusive. I am grateful for the opportunity to share with you my spiritual legacy in these timely tales for the living of these days. May the wisdom and occasional wit of these tales contribute to your journey with and understanding in century 21. If you are so inclined after reading and reflecting on these wisdom tales, you may wish to start a group with others to reflect on these spiritual truths for the living of these days.

Michael D. Dent

Introduction

For 44.5 years, I had the privilege of serving as a pastor in The United Methodist Church. In congregations in Texas and Colorado, large and small, rural, urban, and suburban, new and old, it was my joy to baptize, teach, counsel, confirm, marry, remember the saints, visit the sick, and celebrate worship. When a new pastor is sent to a congregation, the key question on the minds of the pastor's members is, "Can he connect people to Christ, helping them understand Jesus for the living of these days? Can she communicate what it means to comprehend the call of the Christ of God in the present age?" To cut to the chase, can he or she preach?

In over 2,000 messages in the Unites States and overseas, from a teenager to a keen-ager, I sought to share timeless and timely words of God in wisdom tales to serve the current era. These understandings of Jesus call us to study, pray, seek, and claim the Holy One of God as Lord of life. Ninety-five percent of these Bible studies arose from wisdom tales shared over a dozen years in my final pastorate in worship, Sunday school studies, and seasonal small groups.

All but one of these timely tales were shared in worship in the historic Trinity United Methodist Church in the heart of Downtown Denver. Trinity is the oldest congregation in the Mile High City, founded in 1859. Google to glimpse its striking stone steeple soaring almost 200-feet above the sidewalk where tens of thousands of souls pass by each weekday.[1] This holy house of the Lord attracts locals and folks in town for conventions, legislative sessions, athletic contests, concerts, shopping, vacations, and the nearby museums and mountains. On a given Sunday, a billionaire might be sitting next to a homeless person in worship. As in Jesus' day, all the spiritually hungry are welcome to gather, seek, find, and understand Jesus.

The universal drink of hot coffee is served before and after all services. One Sunday every fall, National Football League jersey-clad Kansas City Chief and Denver Bronco fans worship side-by-side in the pews all as God's children. All true Denverites know, however, the Holy One's gridiron preference by the glorious orange and blue sunsets across the Rocky Mountains.

Thanks to a dozen Texas pastoral colleagues with whom I have spent 10 days in Colorado each fall for over 20 years praying, hiking, and sharing food and fellowship. They have helped me understand Jesus across the seasons of life. We work on wisdom texts and tales, sermon series, ideas, themes, texts, outlines, and stories. Special thanks to close colleague Charles Anderson for organizing our trips and sharing keen Biblical insights and illustrations. Charles and I planted new Methodist congregations on the same September Sunday in 1985 in the suburbs of Houston. We have been close friends, encouragers, pilgrims to the Holy Land, and missionaries to Haiti.

I am also grateful to have met, had dinner with, and introduced the Reverend John C. Danforth to the Trinity

1 https://www.trinityumc.org/. Accessed August 31, 2020.

Church family one weekend in August 2016. His record of public service is substantial: Missouri Attorney General, three-term U.S. Senator, U.S. Ambassador to the United Nations, special envoy to Sudan, and ordained priest in the Episcopal Church. You may wish to visit YouTube to see and listen to a timely wisdom tale from the Washington's National Cathedral on September 22, 2019.[2] The guest preacher was none other than former Senator John Danforth. At age 83, the highly respected Republican called on the Cathedral congregation to "Make America **Relate** Again."

I am most humbled and honored to receive Senator Danforth's gracious endorsement of my spiritual legacy. His own legacy of public and spiritual service is remarkable. It is my joy to return the favor and recommend his 2015, still timely work, The Relevance of Religion: How Faithful People Can Change Politics. Danforth remains active in his ninth decade. The John C. Danforth Center on Religion and Politics was established in 2010 and is located on the campus of Washington University in St. Louis. The Center serves as an open venue for fostering rigorous scholarship and informing broad academic and public communities about the intersections of religion and U.S. politics.

2 https://www.youtube.com/watch?v=NGlf-b5l6j8. Accessed August 31, 2020.

CHAPTER ONE

Jesus and Racism

Wisdom Text: Acts 10:23b-36 (The Message)

My great-grandfather was born in Wilkes County, Georgia in 1847. John Taylor Dent enlisted as a teenager in 1863 to fight for the Confederacy in the War Between the States. My ancestor battled to preserve the evil, racist institution which enslaved persons who were brought under the harshest of conditions to this country not to have a better life, but to make life better for others.

The Civil War ended in 1865, but the practice of racism continued. The battle for civil rights for all was not in full swing until almost a century later. Like some of you, I remember separate water fountains, restrooms, and schools for people of color in this country in my childhood years. I recall the overt animosity: indeed, the hatred expressed in the actions and attitudes, the language, and lives of white persons toward black persons. Many of us lived through the tense time of desegregation of public schools, transportation, and lunch counters.

In 2008 the Iliff School of Theology in Denver hosted a community luncheon in honor of the Little Rock Nine. Who were the Little Rock Nine? They were the African-American students who were chosen to integrate all-white Central High School in Little Rock, Arkansas in 1957. The nine endured physical and verbal abuse, being spat on, having acid thrown in their faces, and enduring constant harassing phone calls and death threats.

The President of the United States had to send National Guard troops to protect the courageous students whose only crime was breaking a color barrier declared by the U.S. Supreme Court to be illegal three years before. I cried as I read a book written by one of the nine. Her story shared the chronic anger and abuse each endured and how their faith helped them handle the hate heaped on them day after day for nine months. That student, Melba Pattillo Beals, went on to earn a graduate degree at Columbia University and become a reporter for NBC.

Now fast forward 60 years. In Charlottesville, Virginia, racist actions and attitudes were front and center for the entire world to see. Heather Heyer was one of thousands protesting racism that day in August 2017. The 32-year-old legal assistant was killed when a car was deliberately driven into the crowd. This tragic evil event hit particularly close to home for members of our church family who went to the university there and were married in Charlottesville. We were all shocked and saddened by her death. Heather's goal, her father said, was "to put down hate." Ironically, she was killed by someone filled with hate. The U.S. Attorney General appropriately called her death, "an act of domestic terrorism."

Six months before, I shared a series of wisdom tales from Ecclesiastes called "The Times of Your Life." One of those messages was on the verse, "There is a time to love and a time to hate." I defined hate as "a chronic, intense hostility – the deep emotional aversion often deriving from fear, anger, or a sense of injury." I noted that hate is alive and well in the home of the brave and the land of the free. Recently the

Southern Poverty Law Center – a non-profit organization which combats hate, intolerance, and discrimination though education and litigation – had documented the presence of 892 hate groups in the U.S. These included the KKK, anti-government militias, skinhead, and Aryan nation – some of the same groups present in Charlottesville that fateful day.

Guess what? A week after the killing of Heather Heyer, the SPLC reported there were now 917 such hate groups in this nation. They include Anti-Muslim, anti-LBGTQ, Holocaust Deniers, and White Supremacists. Sixteen of those hate groups were in Colorado. The question we are confronted with is this: "What about racism, hate, and the Christian faith?" Our parents and grandparents may have lived with a "separate but equal" mentality and practice, but those days have run their course and are no longer acceptable among God's people. Separate is never equal.

A statement from the *2016 United Methodist Social Principles* declares, "Racism is the combination of the power to dominate by one race over other races and a value system which assumes that the dominant race is innately superior to all others ... We recognize racism as sin and affirm the temporal worth of all persons ...." In other words, friends, racism is sinful, harmful, and destructive to the soul and body. In a word, racism is evil. Jesus prayed, "Deliver us from evil."

My episcopal leader wrote a blog post in response to the tragic events in Charlottesville. Bishop Karen said, "As a white woman, I have to confront my privilege, and the fact that my walk in the world is much easier because of my race than persons of color. Every day I must confess my racism. Racism is so deeply embedded in our culture and entangles all of us in its web of inequity. I must consciously reject it every day .... The main way I do that is through the power of empathy, listening to how those of color have much different experiences of the world than I do."

What does this mean for us today? I cannot speak for you, but for me there is the need to repent – a need to repent from judgmental and discriminatory attitudes and actions in the past which were inappropriate in the eyes of God. For some of us, there may be a need to reconcile with sisters and brothers whom we have treated unjustly simply because they were different from us. What I am saying is that we need be about healing, restoring brokenness, giving, and receiving forgiveness as needed, and overcoming the pain and hurt from experiences in our younger years when we abused others or were abused by others, over the color of skin.

In the summer of 2016 when police officers were being shot by snipers, our episcopal leader, Bishop Elaine Stanovsky, shared how God was not slow in answering her petition with a call to action. God said, "Hey, church, listen up. Give me some help here. I have prepared you for this. Love your neighbors. Love your enemies. Pray for those who persecute you. Judge not. Cry out for justice. Be my peace-makers."

Then our bishop shared this practice, "When I am buffeted by the news, I turn to scripture in prayer, because I am absolutely certain that God is working through people of faith to build a better future. God wants all people to live in peace and unafraid." Do you believe our Creator desires all folks to not live in fear? The bishop truly laid it on the line.

As I write these words, families of color in Houston and Atlanta have recently buried their sons and brothers killed by the chokeholds and bullets of white police officers. I pray we as a church and as a nation can say "Amen" to Bishop Elaine's vision "to live in peace and unafraid." She also wrote, "Black people and other people of color in America should not be stopped by police, arrested by police, shot by police, die in police custody, given longer sentences, imprisoned or executed at a higher rate than white people".

Racism is evil. Reconciliation is redemptive. For all of us, there is a call to recognize and value all persons as being of sacred worth. We want to look beyond external differences – race, color, gender, sexual orientation, attire, net worth, place of origin, or level of education – and to focus on the sacredness of every human being as God's creation and gift.

Have you ever been to Atlanta? Not far from downtown there is a U.S. National Historic Park which honors the life of the Rev. Dr. Martin Luther King, Jr. In the park is a museum dedicated to the life and work of the civil rights leader. You can tour the church his daddy pastored and in which he preached, along with his childhood home. And of course, there is the crypt which contains his remains.

Martin Luther King, Jr. earned a Ph.D. in systematic theology from Boston University when he was 26 years-old. He was a husband, a father of four, a preacher, an author, a leader in desegregating the South, and a Nobel Peace Prize Winner. Yet, he was despised and hated by many, repeatedly rejected and arrested, covertly investigated, and slandered by his government. Then in April 1968 he was assassinated in Memphis. He was 39 years-old.

A few years ago, I was asked by a thoughtful church member, "Why do we always kill the prophets? Why do we shoot the messenger – Jesus, Gandhi, John F. Kennedy, and Martin Luther King, Jr.?" The answer is: We kill them because they tell us the truth – the truth about justice, about reconciliation, about God and God's vision for humanity and his world.

In his famous speech at the Lincoln Memorial in August 1963, Dr. King shared a dream. His vision expressed this hope, "I have a dream that my four little children will one day live in a nation where they will not be judged by the color of their skin, but by the content of their character."[3]

That is the message of the wisdom tale of this text. Peter, a Jew, stands and speaks to Cornelius and his gentile family members and friends who have gathered. He says, "You know, I'm sure that this is highly irregular. Jews just don't do this – visit and relax with people of another race. But God has just shown me that that no race is better than any other. It's God's own truth, nothing could be plainer: God plays no favorites. It makes no difference who you are or where you are from."

We worship a colorful God. No race or group of people is superior to another in the eyes of God. Do you remember that song many of us learned in Sunday School?

Jesus loves the little children, all the children of the world.
Red and yellow, black, and white, All are precious in his sight.
Jesus loves the little children of the world.

---

3 NPR. "'I Have A Dream' Speech in it's Entirety."
https://www.npr. org/2010/01/18/122701268/i-have-a-dream-speech-in-its-entirety Accessed August 21, 2020.

Those words were written in the 19th century, and they are timeless in their truth that the most important race we belong to is not connected to a color, but one connected to a common Creator.

We are all creatures, *Imago Dei* – made in the image of God. What connects us is our humanity. We all belong to the human race. Color, creed, and cultural differences fall away when deep suffering is shared by fellow members of the human race. God hasten the day when the people of God reflect for the world that the Holy One plays no favorites – that no race is better than any other race. Whether we have been privileged or persecuted because of the pigmentation of our face, we know that our Creator is not concerned about the color of our skin, but the content of our character.

Reflection Questions:

Why is racism unacceptable in the eyes of the Holy One?

Have you been discriminated against because of your color, accent, appearance, gender, or other difference?

Do you need to repent of racist remarks, attitudes, or actions? If so, how so?

How can people of faith bring healing, hope, and help in a time focused on police brutality, Black Lives Matter, systemic injustice, and the legacy of the War Between the States?

What can you do daily to reject racism?

CHAPTER TWO

Jesus and Politics: I Have a Candidate

Wisdom Text: Acts 4:5-12

Every four years, the two major political parties in the United States convene and make the formal selections of their presidential and vice-presidential candidates. The quadrennial gatherings of the Democratic and Republican Parties in two different large American cities in August, bring delegates, supporters, placards, protestors, media, and mountains of money. Having the fortune of attending final evening presidential nominations for both major political parties 16 years apart was incredible, and a surprise both times.

The pass to attend was a last day gift. In 1992, President George H.W. Bush was being nominated for a second term in the cavernous Astrodome in Houston. My laminated guest ticket permitted me to park my posterior on Level 7, Aisle 757, Row 9 in Seat 12. How high was Seat 12 on Level 7? I was even with the beaucoup bags of balloons to be dropped at close of the convention. Over 50,000 rabid Republicans attended the festive event.

My Democratic National Convention experience in Denver in 2008 trumped the Republican gathering as the nomination setting was greatly expanded. After three days of meeting indoors in the 20,000 capacity Pepsi Center, the convention moved outdoors to the Denver Broncos football stadium. I was able to snag ten tickets to share with some pastor friends and my son and his attorney colleagues. It was a memorable, historic evening to witness the first African-American nominee who would be elected President of the United States.

I do not know how you feel about elections, politics, and candidates. I do not know who you may think will make the best leader of the land of liberty, but before I tell you my choice, let me tell you a preacher story. It is a true story about a pastor named Kenneth Goodson. Dr. Goodson was the pastor of the First Methodist Church in High Point, North Carolina over 50 years ago. One fall, there was a prominent U.S. Senator who was a candidate for a national office and who was coming to High Point. Pastor Goodson was intrigued by this candidate and very much wanted to hear him speak, so he called the hotel to inquire about a ticket to the luncheon where the popular senator would be speaking. He was told the tickets were $100 each and was asked how many he wanted. This was a long time ago and $100 was a lot of money for a pastor for a political luncheon. Dr. Goodson wondered what a $100 lunch looked like but declined the opportunity.

He moped around for a few days, but guess what? On the morning of the luncheon, he got a phone call. It seems in all the busy preparations for the event, no one had secured a pastor to pray over the lunch. They asked Dr. Goodson, "Would you be willing to be our guest and to pray?" "Would I be willing to be your guest and to bless the meal? Yes, I would." he replied excitedly. So the pastor got to attend the lunch, offered a prayer, and heard the senator speak. By the way, Dr. Goodson concluded that even for $100, potato salad is still potato salad.

Following the senator's speech, a reporter from the local

newspaper asked each person at the head table one question, "Who is your candidate?" When he came to the pastor, Dr. Goodson replied, "Friend, I am the pastor of the First Methodist Church and I was just asked this morning to come here to pray." "Oh, excuse me, Reverend," the reporter replied and moved on to the next guest and asked the same question, "Who is your candidate?"

Late that afternoon, Martha Goodson, the pastor's wife, went out to get the evening newspaper and was shocked to read what was said about her husband on the front page of the newspaper with the largest evening circulation of any newspaper in North Carolina. There was a picture of the head table. In the accompanying article, the reporter wrote, "Everyone at the head table expressed his choice for a candidate for the office except one person. He was some local preacher there to give the blessing and who apparently had no candidate."

The words stung Pastor Goodson. "Some local preacher there to give the blessing, and who apparently had no candidate."

Brothers and sisters in Christ – Republicans and Democrats and Independents – "I have a candidate." The name of my candidate is not Donald or Joe. No, his name is Jesus Christ of Nazareth. His candidacy is captured in a single sentence by his chief campaign manager, Saul of Tarsus, who proclaims in Philippians 2, "God has given him the name, which is above every name, that at the name of Jesus, every knee shall bow, and every tongue confess that Jesus Christ is Lord …." My candidate is not running for president, but for something far more important: to be Lord of my life, and yours, as well.

Now there are three significant questions we are to ask of any candidate to lead our land or our lives.

Question 1: What has he or she ever done?

My candidate does not score too well here. He was born in an obscure village and placed in a feed trough among animals. There were rumors that he somehow had two fathers. His unmarried mother was a teenager from a peasant family: no pedigree in her family. My candidate grew up in another village and worked as a carpenter until he was 30 years old. Then, he became an itinerant preacher and healer. He never went to college, wrote a book, earned a law degree, owned a home, or set foot in a big city. He never did any of the things which usually accompany greatness. He was never interviewed by Jimmy Fallon or Stephen Colbert, CNN, FOX, or Jimmy Kimmel. He hung out with a dozen guys.

While he was still a young man, the tide of public opinion turned against him. His friends ran away. One betrayed him. Another denied him three times. He went through the mockery of a trial. He was stripped, beaten, and spat on. Finally, he was crucified: a victim of capital punishment. He could have said to his executioners, "When I get home, I'm going to tell my Daddy what you did to me." Instead he prayed, "Father, forgive them, for they do not know what they are doing" (Luke 23:34). He was buried in a borrowed tomb. Stories have it that three days later he was seen walking and talking with his friends.

What has he ever done? Not much, except as a teacher to be the impetus for schools, colleges, and universities around the world. As a healer to be the inspiration for clinics, hospitals, and medical centers named Baptist, Methodist, Catholic,

Lutheran, and Presbyterian.

What has he ever done? He said, "Let the children come. Feed the hungry. Visit those in prison. Care for the dying." He gave marching orders to the Salvation Army, Prison Fellowship, the Little Sisters of the Poor, United Methodist Committee on Relief, Catholic Charities, Lutheran Relief Fund, Prison Fellowship, prison, military, hospice, and hospital chaplains.

What has he ever done? He has changed water into wine, greed into generosity, despair into hope, hate into love, death into life, sadness into joy. He has had more impact on this planet than anyone else who has ever lived. I have a candidate and his name is Jesus. On child abuse and sex trafficking, "Woe to those who cause a little one to stumble" (Matthew 18:6).

On accepting those who are different in age, color, nationality, political, religious, or sexual orientation, "The first and greatest commandment is to love the Lord your God … and the second is like it: You shall love your neighbor as you love yourself" (Matthew 22: 35-40).

On the issue of materialism and greed, "Humans shall not live by stuff alone, but by every word which comes from God" (Matthew 4:4). On the issues of taxes, "Give to the government what belongs to the government...give to God what belongs to God" (Mark 12:17).

Question 2: Where does Jesus stand on the issues of the present day?

You ask him yourself. He has given witness that he opposes those things which bring brokenness, heartache, suffering, and destruction in the human family. My candidate stands in favor of those measures which bring truth, peace, hope, abundance, and harmony for all. He says, "I came that you might have life and have it abundantly." The primary plank of his platform is **LIFE** – abundant life, life eternal, and life in community.

Question Three: The third and final question that must be asked of any candidate today, and especially Jesus: What happens if he wins? What is going to happen if Jesus wins?

- We will have to close many prisons and military bases.
- Many psychiatrists, psychologists, and counselors will see their patient census diminish.
- Divorce and suicide rates will plummet.
- Drug and alcohol abuse will diminish.
- "The lion and the lamb will lie down together" (Isaiah 11:6).
- "We will study war no more" (Isaiah 2:4).
- There will be no more hunger or abused children or terrorist attacks.

If all that sounds too far-fetched, let me pose the question another way: What if Jesus loses? I hate to imagine, I cannot imagine a world without a Redeemer, a Savior, a Son sent to serve and to save and to seek the least, the last, and the lost. That is the self-proclaimed mission statement of my candidate: *To seek and to save the lost, to give his life for the world.*

I have a candidate. His name is Jesus. He is in contention every day to be the Master, Lord, Redeemer, Ruler, strength, and hope for our lives. In our creeds and our prayers, we call Jesus "our Lord." God has made him Lord. Even when we fall and stumble, he forgives us, picks us up, dusts us off, and loves us with an everlasting grace and mercy. There has never been anyone else like Jesus.

The 2016 Summer Olympic Games were held in Rio de Janeiro, Brazil. Over 11,000 athletes from over 200 nations gathered to compete in over 300 events in 28 different sports. On the front page of the of *Denver Post* was an article entitled, "Now we are representing 60 million." It shared the tender story of the first-ever Refugee Olympic Team – a team of ten athletes who fled their homes in Syria, the Sudan, the Congo, Ethiopia, and other conflicted lands. Eighteen-year-old Yusra Mardini is a Christian refugee. In 2015, she was swimming for her life.

An awesome picture of Yusra and the other joyous members of the Refugee Olympic Team was in newspapers around the world. The Refugee Olympians are strategically posed beneath the outstretched arms of Jesus Christ in the 98-feet tall famed statue called *Cristo Redentor* – Christ the Redeemer. Have you been to Rio? Did you see the 2016 Olympics? You could not miss Jesus. He was shown at least a dozen times every evening. This 700-ton religious icon at the top of Corcovado Mountain welcomed the athletes, media members, and all guests to Rio in person and by worldwide telecommunication.

I do not know who your candidate will be in any election for president or other office, but I do know who is running to be Lord of my life. There is no one else like him. I am going to keep looking to the life and love of Jesus for my salvation, hope, and eternal life. I invite you to join me in casting your ballot for Jesus every day in how we live, love, listen, give, pray, and serve.

Reflection Questions:

How do you choose your candidates in political contests?

Have you ever campaigned in a political race?

How is the Holy One of God competing to be Lord of your life?

Who or what is competing to be Lord of your life?

CHAPTER THREE

Jesus and Politics: How Faithful People Can Change Politics

Wisdom Text: Romans 12:9-18

John Danforth was born in 1936 in St. Louis. He earned an undergraduate degree in sociology at Princeton and then attended law school at Yale. At age 32, he was elected attorney general of Missouri. The "Show Me" state sent him at age 40 to Washington D.C. where he served eighteen years in the U.S. Senate before choosing not to run for a fourth term. The moderate GOP leader was once asked why he joined the Republican Party. He answered, "For the same reason you choose which movie to see – it was the one with the shortest line." His public service continued as he was appointed by the President to serve as U.S. Ambassador to the United Nations, and later as special envoy to Sudan. In 2000, he was a finalist for selection as the Vice President nominee of the Republican Party.

What distinguishes John Danforth from most every other elected leader in our nation over the past 244 years is that he is a clergyperson – he holds not only a law degree from Yale University, but also a theological degree from Yale Divinity School. Danforth is, in fact, an ordained priest in the Episcopal Church of America. You might recall that it was Reverend Danforth who presided over the funeral of President Ronald Reagan in the National Cathedral in Washington, D.C. in the summer of 2004.

Reverend Senator Danforth has remained an active and

respected political and spiritual voice in the nation, writing pieces for the op-ed pages of the New York Times and Washington Post. In 2015, he joined 299 other Republicans in signing and sending to the U.S. Supreme Court a friendly brief on behalf of marriage equality. That same year, Senator Danforth wrote a significant book entitled *The Relevance of Religion,* subtitled *How Faithful People Can Change Politics. The Washington Post* calls it "Essential reading for Americans trying to move beyond the corrosive standoff between the religious right and the secular left." *Booklist* notes, "This incredibly thoughtful book will give pause to readers of all political and religious beliefs."

Having been a Danforth Award Recipient in my high school senior year, sharing dinner with him, and preaching with him in the Trinity United Methodist Church congregation in 2016, I am pleased to share four specific ways this highly regarded and respected public servant refines his political and ministerial experience and expertise.

FIRST, we should insist politics remain in its PROPER PLACE. Every four years, we U.S. citizens are privileged to share in the process of picking persons to lead us in the statehouse to the White House. Unfortunately, accusations, innuendos, and rhetoric have reached malignant levels of toxicity. We are simultaneously repulsed by and fixated on what is going to come next in the political campaigns and commentaries. As emotionally invested as we may be in what happens in our national election cycles each two-to-four years, we are wisely reminded by Senator Danforth that politics "is not the realm of absolute truth and is not the battleground of good and evil."

The bottom line is this: People of faith worship God. People of faith do not worship political parties, platforms, or platitudes. Politics is important, but not ultimate. In his 35-page chapter entitled "Politics Is Not Religion," the priest-politician writes these wise words:

> *Politics is a mixture of principle and practicality, of public service and personal ambition. Politics is about power balanced among interests and enforced by government.*

As we have seen recently in 2020 in the cries of "I can't breathe", scathing reports, and racial unrest in many major police departments, sometimes power gets perversely out of balance.

The language of religion is strong, straightforward, uncompromising, and challenging. It puts us in our place and calls us to sacrifice. Whatever we might think about it, one thing should be clear: Politics is not religion, although we often act as though it were. Theologian Paul Tillich pictured faith as the way we order our priorities. Faith expresses our "ultimate concern." Senator Danforth cuts to the chase when he contrasts the hours we spend at worship with the hours we spend working ourselves into a lather watching 24-hour news channels, because it's difficult to claim that God is our ultimate concern, the center of our being, when politics claims so much of our time and our emotions.

The Senator suggests it would be good for us to re-orient our lives, "to spend more hours at worship and fewer in front of the TV… more time in prayer and less time in a rage." Politics is important, but not ultimate. People of faith can change politics by keeping proper perspective. God alone is infinite, transcendent, holy, and worthy of our highest allegiance, sacrifice, and praise.

SECOND, we should be advocates for the COMMON GOOD. The common good focuses on what is in the best interest of all. The Apostle Paul put it this way in Philippians 2:4, "Let each of you look not to your own interests, but to the interest of others." The first verse in the wisdom text tells us to "Hold fast to what is good." Other commands in Romans 12 instructing toward the common good include, "Love … serve … bless … be patient … contribute … feed … give … overcome evil with good." Senator Danforth expresses it this way:

> *Because the essence of religion is that the self is not the center of the universe, and because the model of Christianity is sacrificial love, religion can restore the lost principle that there is a higher good than the self.*

Many followers of Jesus embody a commitment to the common good by sharing their time, talent, and treasure in both seen and unseen ways. Disciples donate school supplies, tutor students, fill boxes with clothing, and donate other items basic to human well being.

One quiet disciple at Trinity Church who gives regularly is a retired college professor. One day, Dr. Phil emailed one of his pastors to tell her that though he woke up grumpy on Monday with some irritating pains, he did not want to miss the food packing party. He later wrote to Pastor Miriam,

> *It was gratifying to deliver the donations to the St. Francis Center … Delivering 743 pounds of food to Metro Caring was a new experience. As we walked through the halls, I had a religious experience, a subjective feeling of oneness with the world. In words that came to me, 'I am among good people doing good work.'*

The Bible says, "Jesus went about doing good" (Acts 10:38).

Religion in general and Christianity in particular advocates for the common good, John Danforth notes, because "the essence of religion is that the self is not the center of the universe, and because the model of Christianity is sacrificial love." Religion can restore the lost principle that there is a higher good than self.

THIRD, we should be a UNIFYING FORCE, working to bind America together. We know well the power of religion to divide and destroy: Sunni and Shiite Muslims in Iraq and Protestant and Catholic Christians in Northern Ireland. The words "ligament" and "religion" come from the same root meaning "to bind together." Jesus prayed for his followers to be one. Paul told the Colossian Christians that in Christ "All things hold together" (Colossians 1:17). Yes, we have diversity in faith communities and in local congregations. Yet, we are united in Christ. In this nation we have much diversity. Yet, as every single U.S. penny, nickel, dime, and quarter declares not only "In God we trust," but also "E pluribus Unum" – "Out of many, one." That is our official U.S. Motto on the Seal of the United States. We pledge our allegiance as "one nation, under God, indivisible…."

Religion is communal. It has the power to bring us together. In a world where many are often wearing headphones or gazing at a screen, or are texting, tweeting, or talking into a portable electronic device, there is something sacred and special to gather in a holy space to encourage and be encouraged, to bless and to be blessed, and to connect our souls with the Divine Creator in praise, prayer, and proclamation.

In early September 2016, Trinity Church launched a mid-week community experience where persons of all ages could gather together to eat, study, sing, ring, learn, worship, meditate, create, and share faith and fellowship. There was place for all at the Wednesday Night Live Family Dinner Table – just as there is a place for all at the Lord's Table every Sunday.

On Sunday, September 11, 2016 in Civic Center Park, three blocks from Trinity Church, there was a remembrance of the attack on America fifteen years before. Over 10,000 persons attended the event, similar to the one five years before when Christian, Jewish, Islamic, and Buddhist clergy participated in the ceremony, as did the Beach Boys. Faithful people were bound together in prayer, music, community, silence, tears, and good vibrations.

Now the fourth and final fundamental concept faithful people of all political persuasions can agree on: We should advocate political COMPROMISE and make the case that the spirit of compromise is consistent with our faith. Senator Danforth writes that "workable politics is the art of compromise – and that the result of inflexible positions is gridlock." I sometimes say of my marriage of 46 years, "Sharon and I have a give and take relationship: I give, and she takes." The reality, of course, is we both compromise. We listen to and respect each other. And sometimes we vote for different candidates.

The lack of compromise in politics leads to polarization. Whether it is Donald Trump or Joe Biden, it takes two poles to polarize. Reverend Danforth calls us all to two religious principles which can make compromise possible – the Second Commandment and Love Commandment. "You shall make no idol" is number two of the Ten Commandments. If we elevate a political ideology to a supreme, non-negotiable absolute place where only the one Holy God belongs, we have entered the world of idolatry. "We must not place on our self-made altars our own perception of truth," Priest Danforth warns. "And we should be especially wary when our perception of the truth coincides, as it often does, with our self-interest." The commandment to love our neighbors as ourselves calls us to listen to, respect, and even seek compromise with those who have a differing political position.

So to bring this home:

- Religion puts politics in its proper place because God alone is transcendent.
- Religion raises our sights above the interest of self and group to the common good.
- Religion is communal and binds us to each other and to the whole.
- Religion creates the environment where compromise can thrive.

Episcopal Priest and former three-term U.S. Senator, Missouri Attorney General, and U.S. Ambassador to the United Nations, The Honorable John Danforth concludes his book, *The Relevance of Religion,* "Faithful people have much to offer to American politics, much that can mend what is obviously broken. But to make this offering, we will have to show up and speak up." As people of faith, we have the power to make a difference for the common good.

Reflection Questions:

What 2-3 things can one do to keep politics in its proper place?

In a season of political polarization in the nation, how does one advocate effectively for the common good?

How can people of faith in such a divided land become a uniting force across 50 red, blue, and purple states?

How can we restore political compromise as a valuable tool in the political toolbox of Democrats, Republicans, and Independents?

Who and what would Jesus vote for?

CHAPTER FOUR

Looking for Transformational Leaders

Wisdom Text: Romans 12:1-8

Not long ago a corporate executive announced the establishment of an annual "Better Leadership Award." The inaugural honor was a posthumous award as the first recipient was Christopher Columbus. The Italian-born explorer who crossed the Atlantic Ocean four times to the Americas was selected for this new leadership recognition for three reasons: 1) He started out not knowing where he was going; 2) when he arrived, he did not know where he was; and 3) upon returning he did not know where he had been. I hope I never win that leadership award. The fact is leadership is a great need in every congregation, community, and country. There are 10,000 books in print with the word "leadership" in their title. There are some 390,000 websites devoted to leadership. Type in the word "leadership" in your computer search engine and you will discover 840 million results.

Every 2-4-6 years we elect leaders in our community, state, and nation. Every fall, churches elect new leaders for their congregations. Leadership is important in the church house, as it is in the White House. For many years, Trinity Church in Denver has offered a course called "Transformational Leadership." That course is connected to the congregational mission statement, "To offer a welcoming and transforming experience: the love of Jesus Christ."

In the wisdom text, Paul calls for us to "not be conformed to this world but be transformed by the renewing of our minds." Transformation means a conversion, and a change, in the case of the text, a new mindset – a fresh vision and outlook on life – no longer business as usual, or conformity to the ways of the world.

In the title of his 2007 book, Lee Iacocca asked the penetrating question, *Where Have All the Leaders Gone?* Not where have all the elected officials gone, not where have all the candidates gone, BUT where have all of the leaders gone? Those persons who can truly make a difference, who can bring needed transformation, hope, and discernment of what is, in the words of verse two, "good and complete and acceptable."

Transformational leaders. That is what we want, need, and are looking for in the church house, the state house, and the White House. The wise passage text teaches us a trio of truths about transformational leaders.

Truth #1: Transformational leaders are committed to the COMMON GOOD. Most of us are familiar with the phrase, "the common good," but do you know where it comes from? It goes back at least 2,500 years in the First Testament story of Nehemiah. He led a campaign to rebuild the wall around Jerusalem. The wall had been destroyed, leaving the city defenseless. Under Nehemiah's transforming leadership, the people gather and decide with one voice, "Let us start building." In the next sentence the storyteller writes, "So they committed themselves to the common good" (Nehemiah 2:18).

The common good is what is beneficial for the community as a whole. Paul described the faith community in today's text as a body – a body with many members, with many parts, but one body – with all of the parts being members of one another. We belong to each other. We try to seek what is best for the whole in our life together as a church, and sometimes that is not easy.

We know our American society has always had ambivalence about the agendas and rights of individuals and those of the community. In his bestseller *Habits of the Heart,* sociologist Robert Bellah examined this tension between public and private allegiance. He concluded that to live a morally coherent life, one must be in community with others, that individual pursuits are inadequate to fulfill us ultimately. The focus of a transformational leader is not on what is best for him or her, but on what is best for the congregation, the community, or the country. A transformational leader does not ask, "What's in this for me?" A transformational leader asks, "What's in this for us?" Paul writes in verse 6, "We have gifts that differ according to the grace given to us." The skill set a leader may be gifted with is not for the sake of the leader, but for the sake of those she or he leads. Transformational leaders are committed to the common good.

The second truth of transformational leaders is this: They are DILIGENT IN LEADERSHIP. When Paul speaks of the gifts of the community, he includes leaders on the list. What he says about leaders is that they possess "diligence." Someone who is diligent is dedicated, vigilant, steadfast, and strong. Diligent leaders persevere in good times and bad. Winston Churchill said, "Success is never final, and failure is never fatal. It is courage that counts." A leader who can bring change is a leader characterized by courage, willing to withstand the criticism and cynicism of others.

Theodore Roosevelt, the youngest man ever to serve as President of the United States, said in a speech in Paris in 1910, following his eight years in office, "It is not the critic who counts, not the man who points out how the strong man stumbled, or where the doer of deeds could have done better. The credit belongs to the man who is actually in the arena, whose face is marred by dust and sweat and blood, who strives valiantly, who errs and comes short again and again, who knows the great enthusiasms, the great devotions, and spends himself in a worthy cause, who at best knows achievement and who at the worst if he fails at least fails while daring greatly so that his place shall never be with those cold and timid souls who know neither victory nor defeat."

Former U.S. Congressman and U.S. Senator from Texas, colleague of John Danforth for 18 years in the Senate, U.S. Secretary of Treasury, and Vice-Presidential candidate Lloyd Bentsen died in 2006. I had met Lloyd Bentsen years before. I knew Lloyd Bentsen. He was my friend. I attended his memorial service at First Presbyterian Church in Houston in May 2006. Presidents, cabinet members, governors, congressmen, senators, and prominent business leaders were present and served as honorary pall bearers. Bush, Clinton, Kissinger, Greenspan, Dukakis, and Baker were all there.

What drew this solemn assembly of Republicans and Democrats to church that Tuesday? It was because Lloyd Bentsen was a diligent leader from his World War II days as a Distinguished Flying Cross winning bomber pilot promoted to the rank of major and commanding a squadron of 600 at age 23, to his service as Secretary of the Treasury in his seventies when he oversaw an economic recovery which created over five million new jobs. Transformational leaders are diligent, courageous, steadfast, strong, vigilant, and highly dedicated. They do not give out, give up, or give in.

The third truth of such leaders is that they are open to being TRANSFORMED themselves. They are willing to grow, change, and mature. Paul has stated in verse two that we are to be "transformed by the renewing of our minds." In the very next verse, he tells us how: "I say to everyone among you not to think of yourself more highly than you ought to think, but to think with sober judgment ..." (Romans 12: 2-3).

We are changed by new ways of thinking and one of those ways is with humility. Humility for a leader means listening to others (including one's critics), learning from one's mistakes, and being truthful about one's shortcomings. No leader has all the answers or all of the truth. A close-minded leader is an oxymoron. Being open to creative ideas, new ways of doing things, and alternative approaches to resolving conflict can lead to the rebirth, the conversion, and the transformation of one's mind, heart, and life.

King David was a leader who harmed others deeply by his selfish, dysfunctional behavior. He hurt his family, friends, and heavenly Father. Yet, in Psalm 78:72, the author concluded with this affirmation of David's eventual leadership of his people: "With an upright heart he tended them and guided them with a skillful hand." King David, the adulterer, was eventually praised for his transformational leadership.

This wisdom tale is not just about candidates for elective office. Not all leaders are high-profile, high-paid, or high-powered. Leaders are parents, teachers, little league and soccer coaches, scoutmasters and den mothers, Sunday school teachers and youth workers, PTA committee members, community liaisons, and members of Rotary Clubs, sororities, community associations, and other volunteer organizations.

In giving, serving, sharing, caring, and yes, leading, we are transformed. Jesus said, "The greatest among you is the one who serves. No one has greater love than this than to lay down one's life for one's friends" (John 15:13). Jesus, the ultimate transformational leader, knew that new life, true life, and transformed life come from serving, self-giving, and the willingness to sacrifice one's life and one's goods.

Unless there is a pandemic, every four years for just over two weeks, billions of persons around the world watch the Summer Olympic Games telecast. The most recent 2016 contests were telecast from Rio de Janeiro, Brazil. I do not know what the highlight of the Olympics may have been for you – maybe seeing the image Christ the Redeemer from various angles in each telecast – you could not get away from Jesus in Rio.

The highlight of the Summer Olympics in Beijing in 2008 for many global citizens had nothing to do with medals, contests, or athletics at all. It had to do with the Opening Ceremonies, Friday, August 8: 8-8-08. Over 200 nations marched in the Olympic stadium known as the "Bird's Nest." The highlight was not the $100 million fireworks show. It was not the presidents, premiers, and powerful national leaders assembled.

No, the most emotional and memorable highlight came with the entry of the host country's contingent. Over 600 athletes from the People's Republic of China were the final team to enter the stadium. The roar from the 91,000 spectators was deafening. Leading the Chinese Olympians was one of the most recognizable athletes on planet earth: basketball player Yao

Ming of the Houston Rockets, all 7'6" of him, or 229 centimeters.

Do you remember that when Yao Ming walked in, he was not by himself? Beside him was a precious, petite child, nine years old, named Lin Hao, with a prominent scar on his scalp, smiling and waving and carrying a tiny Chinese flag. He was too young to be an Olympian. Why was he there? Little Lin was from Wenchuan, the epicenter of an earthquake that killed 70,000 persons three months before. Twenty of Lin Hao's thirty second-grade classmates were killed in the 8.0 magnitude quake on May 12. Lin Hao extricated himself from the rubble that day and went back to where the others were. He saved the lives of two of his classmates. He led the other survivors in singing songs to keep their spirits up while rescuers worked to free them.

The child risked his life because he was their hall monitor. It was his job to lead, and lead he did. When it is our turn to lead, may we lead for the common good. May we lead with diligence. And may we lead with the openness to be transformed. And who knows? Somebody's life may be saved – somebody's soul – maybe our very own.

Reflection Questions:

What does it mean to be committed to "the common good?"

How do diligence, humility, and service contribute to a leader's effectiveness?

What transformational leaders have you known?

How open are you to being transformed as a person and a leader?

CHAPTER FIVE

Jesus and the Jews: What About Our Jewish Friends?

Wisdom Text: Romans 11:1-2a, 29-32

I do not know what it was like where and when you grew up, but I had virtually no contact with Jewish people as a child and teenager. It was not until seminary at Southern Methodist University in 1975 when I took a course in Contemporary Judaism from Rabbi Levi Olan that I came to appreciate the traditions, history, and beliefs of the Jewish faith. The beloved, aged rabbi, known as "the conscience of Dallas," had many of us Methodist ministers-in-the-making almost ready to convert.

My connection with Judaism was significantly strengthened from 1992-1996 when our family lived in a Methodist parsonage in a predominately Jewish neighborhood in Southwest Houston. Our across the street and both next door neighbor families were all Jewish. One was a retired rabbi. Our children went to public schools which had 40 percent Jewish student bodies. Our son graduated from Bellaire High School, affectionately known as "Hebrew High." My ten years in Tyler, Texas brought the blessings of numerous Jewish friends in neighborhood, community, and business organizations. Many of us likewise have Jewish friends, business associates and neighbors. Several of my congregations across the years have had Jewish family members.

The question raised in the wisdom tale is this: What about

our Jewish friends? What is their fate? What is their future? What connection is there between their faith and ours? What kind of relationship is there, and should there be, between Christians and Jews?

Paul wrestles with these questions in his letter to the Romans. Some of us have struggled with them over the years. In a nutshell: Has God turned his back on his chosen people? And for Paul, that question is not just about friends, but about family. After asking that very question in the opening verse of Romans 11, he reminds his readers, "I myself am an Israelite, a descendant of Abraham, a member of the tribe of Benjamin."

In other words, the question is: What is the relationship between the people of God in the synagogue and the people of God in the church? The only honest way we can begin to answer such a question is to confess that the Christian community has a long and well documented history of misunderstanding and mistreating human beings of the Jewish faith. The early church came to blame the Jews for the death of Jesus and to poison the minds of its members. John Chrysostom, a prominent fourth century church leader, asked, "Why are Jews degenerate? Because of their odious assassination of Christ. It is the duty of Christians to hate Jews. The synagogue is a house of prostitution, the domicile of the devil, an assembly of criminals."

Erasmus of Rotterdam would say centuries later, "If it is Christian to hate Jews, then we are all good Christians." A highly selective reading and twisting of Second Testament scriptures yielded such anti-Semitic attitudes. Those attitudes contributed to Christian crusades, inquisitions, and pogroms across the centuries. The escalating intolerance and persecution of Jews across the past 2,000 years has to be disturbing to us all. For centuries, the message of Christians to Jews was this, "You can't live with us as Jews – you have to be baptized." Then the message became, "You can't live with us at all – you have to move into ghettos." Then the message of rejection and hatred reached its horrid highpoint under Hitler. Much of the church was silent when the message became, "You can't live at all – to the gas chambers and incinerators you will go."

Our next door neighbor in Houston for four years was a Holocaust survivor. Her story is told in the National Holocaust Museum in Washington, D.C. Alice Lok was 15 when she and her sister Klara were torn away from their Hungarian family and taken to Auschwitz. There they offered Sabbath prayers in the corner of the camp latrine. Alice's sister was taken away one day, and she never saw Klara again. You can see Alice Lok Cahana interviewed in Steven Spielberg's 1998 Oscar-winning documentary movie, "The Last Days."

If you think anti-Semitism on the part of Christians and society ended with the murder of six million persons in the Holocaust, think again. Do you remember several decades ago when the president of the largest Protestant convention in the United States made the audacious assertion, "God Almighty does not hear the prayer of the Jew"? What message is sent by such an arrogant statement by a high-profile Christian leader?

Several years ago in Sacramento, three synagogues were fire-bombed. Two months later, a mass shooting took place at a Jewish Community Center in Los Angeles. The confessed shooter of three young boys said he wanted his act to be "a wake-up call to America to kill Jews."

The hearts of God and God's people everywhere must break and ache at such hatred. At the same time, we must confess that for centuries the Christian church has contributed consciously or unconsciously by its words and by its silence. Violence against Jews in the name of Jesus is one of the darkest chapters in the history of the church. We need to repent of that sin and rebuild bridges between Jewish and Christian communities.

Norman Ewer remarked, "How odd of God to choose the Jews." Years later Cecile Brown came up with this insightful rejoinder, "But not so odd, As those who choose a Jewish God, But spurn the Jews."

Which leads us to the second major insight of Jewish-Christian relations: We celebrate the fact that we share with our Jewish friends so much: common history and hymns, scriptures and stories, prophets and prayers, covenants and commandments, and, indeed, faith in the one and same God.

The God of Abraham, Isaac, and Jacob and the God of Jesus Christ are not two different gods. They are the one eternal Creator and Redeemer who calls God's people to lives of justice, compassion, righteousness, holiness, repentance, and faith. Jews and Christians both share and affirm the Hebrew commandments to love the Lord our God with heart, mind, soul, and strength, and to love our neighbors as ourselves.

Those commands are from the Torah, the Jewish law. Jesus affirmed them both as central to his teaching. It is incumbent on us as Christians to recognize that two-thirds of our Bible is Hebrew scripture, that not only were Paul and Peter and the first Christians all Jews, but so was Jesus. Jesus was born of a Jewish woman, of the seed of David and the people of Israel.

Christianity began as a Jewish sect. There would be no Christianity without Judaism. As Fred Craddock says, "You don't throw the mother away when the child is born."

Therefore, we need to value, to understand, to respect, and to appreciate our Jewish friends and their faith: a faith tradition that has continued to grow and change and mature since the days of scripture. There are many kinds of Jews: orthodox, conservative, reformed, secular, and messianic. For us to assume all Jews are a certain way is as dangerous as to assume that all Christians are alike.

Now all of this is really still preliminary to the basic question of Romans 11:1,"Has God rejected his chosen people?" And what is the answer Paul gives in the same verse? "By no means."

For two chapters, the Apostle has agonized on the fate of his Jewish friends and family. He has lamented, asked questions, quoted scripture, argued this and that in dealing with the reality that the Jews who were once on the inside are now on the outside, and the Gentiles who were once on the outside are now on the inside. And though the elect of God have been disobedient, unfaithful, and have stumbled on the steppingstone of Jesus Christ, something good has come of it all. As Paul says in 11:11, their stumbling has allowed salvation to come to the Gentiles.

Does that mean that the Jews are now out of the salvation picture? Again, Paul proclaims a resounding "No." He declares in 11:29 that "God's gifts and calling to the Jews are IRREVOCABLE." Do you know what "irrevocable" means? It means incapable of being revoked, changed. Eugene Peterson translates this portion of Romans 11 this way: "From your point of view as you hear and embrace the good news of the Message, it looks like the Jews are God's enemies. But looked at from the long-range perspective of God's overall purpose, they remain God's oldest friends. God's gifts and God's call are under full warranty – never canceled, never rescinded."

Paul reminds his Christian readers not to boast or to be arrogant in their relationship to God through Christ. Christianity, he says, has been grafted as a wild olive branch to share the rich faith root of the olive branch which is Judaism. And though lack of belief has caused some of the branches to be broken off, God still desires to graft those branches back into the tree as well. Paul says in 11:18, "Remember, you don't support the root, the root supports you – the root of Abraham, Isaac, and Jacob."

The biblical bottom line: We all rejoice in our salvation as a gift from a merciful and gracious God, received through faith. The overriding message of the Apostle is a message of mercy. Nine times in Romans 9-11 he uses the word "mercy" or "merciful," three times the word "kindness," and four times the word "grace."

His message of divine mercy crescendos in verse 32, "For God has imprisoned all in disobedience (Jew and Gentile) so that he may be merciful to all." Merciful to all. Earlier in 10:12, Paul writes, "For there is no distinction between Jew and Greek; the same Lord is Lord of all and is generous to all who call on him." Before that in 9:18, "So then God has mercy on whomever he chooses ...."

What Paul is saying is simply this: God is God and we are not. God created us: we did not create God. God chose us: we did not choose God. God is free to save whom he will. God saved us: we did not save ourselves. God is merciful and, indeed, desires to save the world.

A popular hymn decades ago proclaims, "There's a wideness in God's mercy, like the wideness of the sea ... there's a kindness in God's justice, which is more than liberty."[4] God's mercy is for all: it is inclusive and not exclusive. For me, that mercy came in a person called Jesus: he is the embodiment of grace. He is the one I must bear witness to at all times and in all places as the Christ, as the Messiah, as my Lord and my Savior. Can I exclude my Jewish friends from the rich love, the deep mercy, and the amazing grace of God? Of course not. None of us can limit the love of God, whose mercy is for all.

Whether that mercy of God will be experienced in Christ for all persons or not, I cannot say. What we can say is that God will never stop working to win his people to faith, to save them through his eternal mercy. Neither we nor Paul can explain what he calls in 11:33 the "unsearchable judgments and inscrutable ways of God." What we know for sure is this: God's grace is utterly amazing: and is free for all, and available for all.

---

4 Frederick William Faber. "There is a Wideness in God's Mercy." https://hymnary.org/text/theres_a_wideness_in_gods_mercy. (Public domain. Accessed August 24, 2020).

Reflection Questions:

How many Jewish neighbors, friends, or classmates did you know growing up?

How were the relationships between Jews and Christians in your community?

How have your perception of Jewish-Christian relationships changed as you matured?

What new insights in Jewish-Christian relations did you gain in this wisdom tale?

CHAPTER SIX

Jesus and Other Religions: One Way or Many?

Wisdom Text: Acts 17:16-28

Have you ever gone back in time? If you have not, all you have to do is travel to St. Simons Island, Georgia. That is where I went many years ago for a family wedding. It was like going back to my childhood over 50 years ago in Southeast Texas. Why would I say that? Because it seemed in every other block on the island there was a Christian church: Baptist, Methodist, Lutheran, Presbyterian, Catholic, Community, and Church of Christ. Not only was St. Simons a highly Christian setting, but it was distinctively Methodist. There were two sizable United Methodist congregations, two Methodist retirement communities, a fifty-acre Methodist campground which can accommodate 1,000 overnight guests, and a Wesley Memorial Garden to honor the lives of John and Charles Wesley, Methodism founders who preached on St. Simons in 1736, over 280 years ago.

I do not know where you grew up, but if you are over 65 years old and grew up in this country, you may have thought it was a Christian nation. We said the Lord's Prayer every day in public school. Most everybody we knew was a member of some church. We may have had a Jewish acquaintance or two if we lived in a larger community.

In 1955, Will Herberg published the first edition of his classic essay in American religious sociology. Do you remember its title? *Protestant-Catholic-Jew.*

Guess what? The world has changed in the past half-century. The American religious scene is no longer exclusively Protestant, Catholic, and Jewish. Many of us grew up never encountering a single Buddhist, Hindu, or Muslim. President John Kennedy's policy reforms shifted the patterns of immigration. Immigrants began arriving from Asia and the Middle East. Mosques, pagodas, and temples began showing up across the main streets of America. After the fall of communism, other major religions became more visible on the world stage. The Dalai Lama brought Buddhism to a wider audience. The staggering revival of Islam grabbed the world's attention. A Hindu nationalist party seized leadership in India.

Today there are about seven billion human souls in the world. Two billion – about 1/3 – profess to be Christian. Around 1.3 billion – or about 20 percent – are Muslim. There are about 900 million Hindus, or 1/7 of the world's population. There are around 360 million Buddhists, or about 5 percent of the planet's people. There are about 14 million Jews in the world. Here in the United States, 77 percent of persons profess to be followers of Jesus, 15 percent claim no religious affiliation, and 1.3 percent are Jewish. Hindus, Muslims, and Buddhists each comprise about one-half of one percent of the U.S. population. However, in the last two decades, Islam, Buddhism, and Hinduism grew respectively by rates of 110, 170, and 237 percent. All of which is to say that the American religious scene has changed dramatically and is still doing so.

The questions we ask are real:

- What about other religions? How do we relate to these other major religions in our midst?
- Are we right in our faith and they are wrong?
- Are we all right and will we all go to heaven?
- Are we all worshiping one God or several? Is there one way or many?

There are three traditional views of how people of the Christian faith view themselves and others. And then conclude how we as United Methodist followers of Jesus are called to connect to our neighbors who may follow Mohammed, Moses, Brahman, or Siddhartha.

The first way for Christians to look at other religions is called the Exclusivist approach. Exclusivists, sometimes called particularists, believe that only those who have faith in Christ can be saved and have eternal life. Without a conscious commitment to Christ, one is lost and cannot receive the salvation. Many of us grew up hearing this message in revivals, from preachers on television, and in our local congregations. No matter how good or spiritual or loving people were who practiced other faiths, they had no hope of heaven without professing Jesus as their Lord and Savior, if they had the chance to do so.

On the downside, there is a sense of spiritual superiority in such a closed system. Across the years, exclusivism at its worst has led to crusades, burning people at the stake, and other radical attempts of forced conversions to the Christian faith. Nonetheless, exclusivists are still a large contingent in the Christian family and are committed to converting the other four billion residents of planet earth to the way of Christ and saving them from the fires of hell. Some of us may well have some exclusivism in our spiritual lineage.

At the other extreme is the Pluralistic perspective. People who are pluralistic believe that all or most all religions are valid, legitimate ways of connecting to Ultimate Reality. A pluralist says:

> *There are many different true paths to God. People should follow the path that works for them. No one path is better than another.*

In other words, salvation is available in any faith community. It is not limited to those committed to Christ. This is a popular view in today's post-modern culture. Openness, tolerance, and acceptance of diversity are highly valued in our society. A nonjudgmental pluralist may say, *Your truth is true for you, and my truth is true for me.* Some of you perhaps consider yourselves pluralists.

I am compelled to cite a couple of challenges to the pluralistic perspective. First, it does not honor various faiths. As Adam Hamilton points out in his book, *Christianity and World Religions,* most Muslims would not feel that we are honoring them by saying that what they believe is as true as what Hindus believe. They would say, at best, we do not understand their faith. If we understood it, we could not possibly say that Islam and Hinduism are equally true pathways to the divine.

Another problem of the pluralist point of view is its failure to differentiate sufficiently between the logic, merit, and validity of competing religious beliefs. If religion is the human response to spiritual yearnings, needs, and experiences, then some of these responses may lead to exclusive faith claims that do harm to other faith traditions or bring destruction to adherents of that faith community. Some religious leaders are charismatic, but deluded individuals. Most of us would agree that religious expressions such as the People's Temple in South America in November 1978 and the Heaven's Gate Hale-Bopp Comet cult in California in March 1997 – both resulting in mass suicide – were not healthy, logical, valid expressions of truth, hope, and wholeness for their followers.

Between the extremes of Exclusivism and Pluralism regarding the world's religions is the Inclusivist Perspective. This perspective takes something from each extreme and creates an attractive middle ground. Christians who are inclusive believe, like exclusivists, that salvation and eternal life come only through Jesus Christ. Jesus is the definitive revelation and expression of God. However, unlike the exclusivists, inclusivists believe that a person who does not know or does not accept Christ can be saved nonetheless through the power of Christ.

To put it another way, a person comes to God exclusively through Christ but he or she has not necessarily trusted in Christ or even heard the name of Christ. Clark Pinnock, a well-known evangelical Christian apologist, author, and professor speaks of pagan saints, persons of great faith of non-Christian religious traditions.

Catholic theologian Karl Rahner writes of the "anonymous Christian" who is saved by Jesus even without consciously knowing Jesus the Christ. The bottom line of inclusivism is that Jesus died for all and that God, in his great mercy, wisdom, and grace, is at work even through the religious practices, faith, and lives of non-Christians to bring them salvation and eternal life.

What I am saying as a Christian about other religions is that God and God's work in the lives of his children of other faiths or even no faith are beyond my ability to comprehend. The text tells us that when Paul came to Athens preaching the gospel, he found a diverse religious expression. He met and discussed with the philosophers and debaters. He met people where they were. He bore witness to Christ, but he did not beat people over the head with threats of hell. He shared the Creator God, the source of life who is near to all, using a line from a Greek poet about God, the one "in whom we live and move and have our being" (Acts 17:28). Paul spoke of repentance, righteousness, and resurrection in the text which follows.

When we step back and see the big picture, the sweeping story of God in the stories of scripture, we discover that God and God's redemptive work are not exclusive, but inclusive of the world's peoples.

- God sent Jonah to preach repentance to the Ninevites in the capital city of the wicked Assyrian Empire.
- God called the Persian King Cyrus his anointed.
- God showed compassion for the rejected Hagar and Ishmael and promised to make them into a great nation, a promise our Arab and Muslim friends believe was fulfilled in them.
- God spoke to Zoroastrian priests – magi – and called them to go and worship the Christ child.
- Jesus said, "I am the way, the truth, and the life. No one comes to the Father but through me – but he also said – I have other sheep that do not belong to this fold. I must bring them also…So there will be one flock, one shepherd" (John 14 and 10).

- Jesus said, "In my Father's house are many rooms ..." (John 14).
- John said of Jesus, "The true light, which enlightens everyone, was coming into the world" (John 1).
- Peter proclaimed, "I understand that God shows no partiality, but in every nation anyone who fears him and does what is right is acceptable to him" (Acts 10).
- Paul wrote, "For to this end we toil and struggle, because we have set our hope on the living God, who is the Savior of all people, especially of those who believe" (I Timothy 4).

So where does this all leave us with regard to our neighbors of other faiths? Whether you name yourself as exclusivist, pluralist, or inclusivist, how do you relate to non-Christian believers? We are not the first to ask those questions. We are most grateful to belong to a faith family which gives guidance for such interfaith relationships. The United Methodist Church Book of Resolutions has far more to say on the subject. Go online for additional resources.

When you scan this document, you discover we are encouraged to do several things in five statements. The call there can be summed in a triad of simple alliterative, achievable actions: Listen to, learn from, and look for common ground with our neighbors of other faiths. In other words, get to know our friends who may approach and experience God and faith in ways different than our own. Visit an interfaith event, study, or dialogue event. We are blessed to live and worship in a nation where such opportunities are readily available.

For United Methodist Christians to dialogue with and witness, in the best sense of the word, to our friends of other faiths, we must know what we believe and why we believe what we believe. We must also examine our lives:

- Is our faith evident in our daily lives?
- Can someone look at us and see the life and love of Jesus Christ manifested in how we live daily?
- Is there prayer?
- Do we share?
- Do we care?

Sometimes we Christians have become quite pre-occupied with the eternal destiny of our non-Christian neighbors, while neglecting the state of our own spirituality.

On the Monday afternoon following the weekend family wedding on St. Simons Island, I was in the Jacksonville International Airport in North Florida with my wife and daughter awaiting our flight to Dallas. I had some extra time, so I went in the airport chapel. It was a non-denominational meditative setting. There was a book on a small desk in which travelers passing through the airport could share their prayers of praise, intercession, and confession. I glanced at the opening sentences of several of those prayers. Most were in English, but not all. They began:

- Holy Lord
- Padre Dios
- Heavenly Father
- Dear Abba
- Hare Krishna
- Mother/Father God

I believe almighty God heard each of those prayers, in whatever language or vocabulary each was prayed. God is bigger than my or your experience of God.

On Tuesday, September 11, 2001, our world changed. Planes crashed into buildings. Innocent citizens of several dozen nations died. Christians, Jews, Muslims, and atheists perished in the collapse of the twin towers. Hundreds of brave firefighters and police officers gave their lives in an effort to save others. And many persons became fearful of their neighbors because of their religion.

The Tyler, Texas Ministerial Alliance was meeting at noon on Tuesday, September 11, 2001. As a result of what we were seeing on the TV screen during our meeting, we decided to have a Community Prayer Service that night. The local TV stations announced it. That night at the First Baptist Church, over 1,000 folks from all faith communities of East Texas came together to mourn, to pray, and to worship. A Baptist presided, a Catholic prayed, a Presbyterian read scripture, and a Methodist and a Muslim spoke in the Baptist pulpit .... And God smiled ... and God wept with his people...all his people...all over his world ... and he still does.

Prayer

God and Father of us all, who is above all and through all and in all, we have come to know you as a God of wide mercy, deep love, and amazing grace ... a God who knows our pain and our joy .... We love you, we trust you, we seek to serve you .... We rejoice that you so loved the world that you gave yourself in your only Son that we might have eternal life ... that you sent your Son not to condemn the world, but that the whole world might be saved through him. Great, indeed, is the mystery of the gospel. In Jesus' name we pray. Amen.

Reflection Questions:

In what kind of religious home were you reared?

What did you learn about other religions?

To which religious bent do you most lean now: Exclusivist, Pluralist, or Inclusivist? Why?

CHAPTER SEVEN

Jesus and Human Sexuality: Bringing the "L Word" Home

Wisdom Text: Matthew 22:34-40

In late April and early May 2008, the General Conference of The United Methodist Church met for ten days in Fort Worth, Texas. Almost 1,000 lay and clergy delegates from across the United States and several other nations discussed, debated, and decided on legislation generated by petitions from individuals, congregations, and annual conferences. I attended several days of the conference as an observer. During the time I was there, the report from the Church and Society Legislative Committee on Human Sexuality was presented.

The report, passed by a 39-27 vote in the committee, recommended removing from our Social Principles a line in the document which reads:

> *The United Methodist Church does not condone the practice of homosexuality and considers this practice incompatible with Christian teaching.*

The report offered a carefully crafted compromise that appeared to meet the needs of the body. Then came a minority report from the legislative committee. Three hours of debate ensued, with several amendments added. Finally, by an exceedingly small margin of votes, the minority report became the majority report and was adopted. The phrase "incompatible with Christian teaching" was retained for another four years. Even a seemingly appropriate amendment to add the words "We agree to disagree in these matters" was defeated by a small margin.

The presiding bishop at that plenary session then called a recess and permitted a witness to be made following the lengthy, heated debate on the issue of homosexuality. Into the convention center marched hundreds of persons dressed in black. Many were parents of gays and lesbians. They carried posters with pictures of their sons and daughters on them – and with each picture was this message, *My Child Is of Sacred Worth.* Others wore t-shirts or buttons or carried posters which tersely declared, *All Means All,* and *Closed Hearts, Closed Doors, We Mind.* Hundreds of delegates on the floor, conference guests in the balconies, and bishops on the platform stood in solidarity with the protestors. Tears rolled down the cheeks of many present as the marchers began to sing softly:

Jesus loves me, this I know
For the Bible tells me so
Little ones to Him belong
They are weak, but He is strong
Yes, Jesus loves me
Yes, Jesus loves me
Yes, Jesus loves me
The Bible tells me so

I share that indelible experience with you to say that when it comes to homosexuality, the house is divided. Three subsequent General Conferences have not resolved the conundrum. The United Methodist Church Social Principles dealing with this topic continue to be a source of not only prolonged debate and discussion, but also deep pain and intense conflict among Methodist Christians of good conscience for over 50 years. I invite you to reflect with an open mind and open heart to the Spirit of God in seriously engaging the topic of homosexuality and ask yourself honestly, What do I believe? Why do I believe what I believe? What does the Bible say about homosexuality? What does it not say? What does the church say? And perhaps most importantly, what does Jesus say about homosexuality, and our neighbors and our family members who are oriented in a same-sex direction? Four realities guide our timely spiritual reflection.

Reality #1: The UMC stands strong for equal rights for all. Our denominational Social Principles clearly say, "Certain basic human rights and civil liberties are due all persons. We are committed to supporting those rights and liberties for all persons, regardless of sexual orientation." I trust this is one thing we can all agree on as a matter of justice. Discrimination is wrong. At least 94% of Fortune 500 companies have non-discriminatory policies regarding gay persons.

The Social Principles states, "We support efforts to stop violence and other forms of coercion against all persons, regardless of sexual orientation." In 1998, a 21-year-old Wyoming college student named Matthew Shepard was tortured and murdered in an anti-gay hate crime. In 2009, a jury in Greeley, Colorado found a young man guilty of committing a hate crime in the killing of 18-year-old transgendered Angie Zapata. Less than a month later, another transgendered woman was brutally attacked, sexually assaulted, and left for dead in a motel room in Trinidad in Southern Colorado. What else but pure, unadulterated hate and fear could motivate one human being to destroy the life of another brutally and violently simply because that person is different?

Words and acts less than purely violent can take their toll, as well. Roger was gay. The boys in his high school all knew it and made his life miserable. When they passed him in the hallway, they called out his name effeminately and made crude gestures. Roger never took showers in PE because he knew his classmates would whip him with wet towels. One day in gym class the guys ganged up on Roger, dragged him into the showers, and shoved him into a corner. Curled up there, this teenager cried and begged for mercy as his five classmates urinated on him. That night Roger went to bed as usual. Sometime around two in the morning he got up, went down to the basement of his house, and hung himself.

Tony Campolo, the teller of that story, was one of Roger's classmates who was not there that day. Tony writes:

> *On that day I realized I was not a Christian. I believed the Apostles' Creed, declared Jesus to be my Savior. But if the Holy Spirit had actually been in me, I would have stood up for Roger. When the guys came to make fun of him, I would have put one arm around his shoulder, waved the guys off with the other and told them to leave him alone, to not mess with him, because he was my friend.*

Then Tony says:

> *But I was afraid to be Roger's friend. I knew that if you stood up for a homosexual, people said cruel things about you, too. So I kept my distance. If I hadn't, who knows if Roger might be alive today.*

In the foolishness of adolescence, probably some of us spoke cruel words or perhaps did stupid things to people because we perceived them to be different – they were a different weight, they were a different color, or they were attracted to someone of the same sex. An active member of my congregation in

Denver wrote me that her husband's sister is gay, as is their daughter. The daughter and her partner lived next door for a while to a family with three boys. The boys tormented the dogs of their lesbian neighbors, stole one of their cars, and spray painted faggot all over the other car.

God forgive us when we have hurt someone with words or deeds because of fear or hate. God forgive us if we damaged or destroyed the soul of another child of God through our mistaken discrimination in the past. God forgive us, for such behavior is sinful and expressive of our own brokenness.

Reality #2: Homosexual orientation is not a choice. To diminish gay persons is to deny what science is discovering. Research is confirming what many have thought for a long time: Persons do not choose to be gay. While no one can presently know precisely what creates sexual orientations, Johns Hopkins University professor and researcher John Money suggests an interaction between biological and sociological influences combine to create homosexual orientation.

If you are heterosexual, did you choose your heterosexual orientation? Or was it just something that came to you without asking, just came naturally that you were attracted to persons of the opposite sex? If it were a choice, why would someone choose an orientation in which he or she would be the object of ridicule and rejection? Another active member of the Trinity Church family wrote me a letter a few weeks ago. She shared that over a dozen years ago over Christmas vacation, her adult son broke the news that he was gay. They both sat and cried. She said, he was so afraid that I would disown him, or tell him that he was not welcome in our home anymore, for that is what happened to several of his friends when they shared that news with their parents.

Then she wrote, "I cried some more and said, 'How could I ever not welcome you? I carried you for nine months and raised you. I love you and you are mine.' I remember him so well saying, 'Why would anyone choose to be gay, when people will hate you, you'll be discriminated against for rights other people take for granted, and worse?' Then he said, 'I did not choose to be gay. God made me this way.'"

Indeed, homosexual orientation is present in between one and ten percent of the population. That means there are between 60 million and 600 million gay persons in our world. No wonder we have gay congressional representatives and singers, doctors and lawyers, teachers and pastors, actors and actresses, athletes and authors. Nowhere does our United Methodist statement disavow homosexual orientation. Our sexuality – whatever direction in which it may be oriented is a mystery. Our orientation is something we did not choose and cannot control. We can control our behavior, but we cannot control our orientation.

In 2008, the American Psychological Association declared that mental health professionals should not tell gay clients that they could become straight through therapy or other treatments. After years of research, the APA puts itself firmly on record that the so-called reparative therapy by conservative religious groups is not only an ineffective approach, but also could be harmful in contributing to depression and suicidal tendencies.

Reality #3: Homosexuality must be viewed in the larger context of our human sexuality. The UMC's position on homosexuality is founded in the section entitled Human Sexuality. Notice also that the section begins with this positive proclamation, "We affirm sexuality is God's good gift to all persons. We call everyone to responsible stewardship of this sacred gift."

We are all the recipients, the beneficiaries of this divine gift called sexuality. God made us and gifted us all with various gifts. Stewardship means we have been entrusted with something to take care of, to nurture, and to use wisely to God's glory. That is why our statement begins paragraph three this way, "We deplore all forms of the commercialization, abuse, and exploitation of sex."

The greatest threat to traditional marriage and family life in America today is what? Not homosexuality. What do you think it is? It is infidelity, cheating, unfaithfulness. The Bible calls it adultery and it is so destructive it made God's Top Ten List. Jesus speaks strong words against adultery in all three synoptic gospels. In 2009, adultery made the cover of TIME magazine. The July 13 issue showed a wedding cake with a bride and groom sinking precariously into the top layer of the cake. Above the couple are the title words, Unfaithfully Yours, and then the sentence, "Infidelity is eroding our most sacred institution." When you turn inside you find pictures of prominent powerful couples in which the husband – be it Governor Mark Sanford, Senator John Edwards, or Governor Eliot Spitzer, has cheated on his wife.

I do not know what you think, but I am deeply saddened and disturbed to see billboards all around that say

1-800-DIVORCE

DIVORCE IN A DAY

The message of these commercials is that marriage is an easily disposable, temporary commodity.

In another gross misuse of the sacred gift of sexuality, roughly 20 percent of teens admit to participating in "sexting," according to a survey by the National Campaign to Support Teen and Unplanned Pregnancy. One in five American teenagers is sending nude or semi-nude photos of themselves to friends on their cell phones. There cannot be anything good coming from that. The truth is this: Whether one is heterosexual or homosexual, the misuse of the good gift of human sexuality is an affront to the Creator. We usually, if not always, end up hurting others, ourselves, or both when we employ this sacred gift in anything but a committed, monogamous, covenant-love relationship.

Which leads us to Reality #4: What the Bible says and does not say about homosexuality and what it means. I hope we mostly all agree on what we have shared so far. What we share now may be a little more challenging for some. I invite you to read with open hearts and open minds, and with spiritual ears.

How many times does the Bible mention homosexuality? Fifty times? Five hundred? A thousand? In one interpretation or another, the Bible mentions the practice of homosexuality a grand total of seven times.

In only a couple of these is there an unequivocal condemnation of the occurrence. Two of those are in the book of Leviticus in the purity code of ancient Israel. This was not the moral code of what was right and wrong, but the code of what was Kosher for orthodox Jews. The verses are Leviticus 18:22 and 20:13. If you look these up, you will see that the penalty for violating the code is death. But you will also notice that other behaviors prohibited in the code include adultery, cursing your father or mother, eating shellfish such as lobster or crab, having relations with your wife during her period, wearing a fabric made of more than one kind of thread, eating pork, and touching the skin of a dead pig. The penalty prescribed for most of these is death. If taken literally, that takes care of playing football with the ole football.

If we look to the Bible for literal guidance on relationships, what we find is the acceptance of these practices: prostitution, polygamy, sex with slaves, concubines, treatment of women as property, and marriage of girls as young as age 12. What we see is that we are on shaky ground trying to build a value system from random texts on homosexuality or any other subject. We have to consider culture, context, time, and place in interpreting the laws, the stories, and the poetry of scripture. We have to seek the Word of God among the words of scripture. We do not worship the Bible, but the Holy One revealed therein.

I have read many books and articles on the Bible, sexuality, and the church. There is obviously no unanimity in this area. Some particularly powerful insights about homosexuality and the Bible came in the words of Lewis Smedes, a highly respected evangelical professor of theology and ethics at the conservative Fuller Theological Seminary for 28 years, and a husband for 50 years. In his article on the book *Homosexuality and the Christian Faith,* Smedes begins:

> *Homosexuality is a mystery. But then heterosexuality is a mystery, too. Reading the creation stories and what the New Testament tells us about marriage and family persuades me that the Creator originally intended the human family to flourish through heterosexual love. But nature has gone awry, as it sometimes does; and it*

seems most reasonable to me to believe that God intends homosexual people to bear their destined burden in as morally responsible a way as they can. And I further believe that a committed partnership of love is one morally responsible way to do so. As far as I can tell, the New Testament gives no specific guidance about the moral choices that gay people should make.

Then Professor Medes goes on to share six significant things about homosexuality that the Bible is silent about.

- The Bible does not tell us anything about a condition called homosexuality.
- The Bible does not tell us how people get to be homosexual people.
- The Bible does not tell us whether homosexuality is "curable."
- The Bible does not tell us what sorts of persons homosexual people are likely to be.
- The Bible tells us that homosexual behavior is unnatural but does not tell us why it is unnatural.
- The Bible does not tell us of the personal quality of homosexual relationships.

I do not know what you believe about homosexuality. The worldwide United Methodist Church continually affirms by smaller and smaller margins each four years that *the practice of homosexuality is incompatible with Christian teaching*. I would add one word to that statement: SOME. Some Christian teaching. In 1995, I preached on this subject. I used phrases I thought were true at the time: *alternative lifestyle, inherently promiscuous,* and *gender disturbance.* I do not know about you, but my mind has changed over time. With deep reflection, study, and prayer, with a richer experience and interaction with a wider variety of persons, I have come to some convictions about Christianity, homosexuality, and the church. You may view some of these differently.

Just as in the past when we have made a grievous mistake in discounting and discriminating against people who were black or red or brown or female or had a handicapping condition or were left-handed, I believe we have erred in the same way with our gay neighbors.

- I believe we need to set aside our fears and prejudices and affirm the presence and gifts of our homosexual neighbors. Many of us have gay family members. My wife and I both do. From the letter I shared earlier written by a woman in our church about her gay sister-in-law and gay daughter and the lives and loves they share, our family and this world are better places with these loving and caring lesbians in it. We cannot imagine it in any other way. They did not choose to be lesbians. They are God's children in my eyes.
- I believe we want to continue to welcome, embrace, and invite our gay friends and all others to follow Jesus, to experience the welcoming love of God in an inclusive church family.
- I believe, above all, we want to walk in the footsteps of Jesus in all relationships. Do you know what Jesus said about homosexuality? Not a single word. He did have a lot to say about self-righteous religious folks judging other people, though. And none of it was pleasant or positive. See Matthew 23.

- As I said earlier, we are all – homosexual and heterosexual – all called to express our sexuality in committed, monogamous, covenant love relationships. Promiscuity is inappropriate for any of us.

One day Jesus was asked what the most important commandment was. He answered, "You shall love the Lord your God with all your heart, and with all your soul, and with all your mind. This is the first and the greatest commandment. Then Jesus said, 'And a second critical commandment is just like it: You shall love your neighbor as yourself. Everything depends on these two commandments'" (Matthew 22:37-40).

One of my friends, a leader in our church, and a faithful disciple of Jesus, sent me an email several years ago. Listen for the poignant pain and the gift of grace:

> *Dear Pastor Mike, here are some of my thoughts and experiences. I hope they may be of some help ... I found the strength to come out at Trinity. I guess in some ways when I finally admitted being gay, the aftermath was like getting a terminal illness. Why me, God? Couldn't you give me something else? I'll do anything to make this go away. I have spent many a tear-filled night asking why. One concept that helped, I learned on the Emmaus Walk. I learned that we are all born broken in some way .... Then this sentence, I know that my church loves me and accepts me as I am.*

I hope and pray you will belong to a church family where the L word, love, the central command of Jesus will be at its center, bringing broken people – all of us – home to God, home to healing and hope and wholeness. I long for the day when we will be more concerned about the spiritual orientation than the sexual orientation of a child of God.

Open heart, open minds, open doors. May it be so. May it be so.

O God, like that mother who told her son, "I love you – you are mine," may we as the body of Christ be the headlight and not the taillight, as we welcome all of your children. We are all broken in some way. Thank you for saving us. In the name of love incarnate, Jesus our Lord, we pray. Amen.

Reflection Question:

Did you have homosexual family members or friends you were aware of as you approached adulthood?

How were they treated by family, church, and classmates?

If any, what message about homosexuality did your congregation send about homosexuality?

What keen insights on same-sex relationships did you gain from this wisdom tale?

CHAPTER EIGHT

Jesus the Refugee

Wisdom Text: Matthew 2:13-23

Millions and millions of folks, perhaps a billion, share in services across the globe lighting candles and singing "Silent Night, Holy Night." The good news of God's coming in the birth of a baby was not good news for everybody, though. King Herod was "troubled" by the news of the newborn king of the Jews. He commanded the Magi to report to him where the newborn boy was so he, too, could go and worship him. The Magi were later warned in a dream not to return to Herod and went home another way.

That is where the wisdom text begins. It is a tough tale, a story of paranoia and violence, of mass execution and great grief. You may never have heard it read. Many pastors take off the Sunday after Christmas and never touch it. Perhaps you have never heard of it.

Baby Jesus is #1 on King Herod's hit list.

This vicious, ugly story consists of three dreams. In the first one, Joseph, the father of Jesus is told by an angel, "Get up. Take your wife and child and escape to Egypt. Stay there until further notice because King Herod is about to search for and kill baby Jesus." Joseph obeys, gets up in the middle of the night, and takes Mary and young Jesus to Egypt.

Meanwhile, Herod realizes the wise men have fooled him and orders his soldiers to go and execute all of the male children in and around Bethlehem ages two years and younger. Scholars estimate that given the population of the community and mortality rate of the time, probably twenty children were put to death in an unspeakable horror that has come to be known as "The Slaughter of the Innocents." That is the same number of children lost in 2012 in another slaughter of innocents in New Town, Connecticut.

Paranoia, fear, and insecurity can contribute to people doing crazy and destructive things. Whether it is the president of North Korea or King Herod in text, male leaders often misuse and abuse their power in eliminating those whom they perceive as threats. Historians tell us that Herod's paranoia had contributed to the execution of three of his own sons. Can you imagine, though, being threatened by a baby born in a feed trough?

And can you imagine the unspeakable grief and hysteria experienced by those mothers and fathers in Bethlehem as Roman soldiers went house to house in Bethlehem neighborhoods carrying out their brutal mission?

In his book, *When Jesus Came to Harvard,* theologian Harvey Cox writes of his sharing of this seldom-read brutal story to an undergraduate class he taught at that prestigious university. A student asked him, "Do you think when he grew up Jesus was told about all the children who died violently because the king was trying to kill him? If he had been told, how did he feel about it?"

Professor Cox pointed out that children often suffer agonizing mental torment when they think they have contributed to someone's death. And, in this case Jesus did, at least indirectly, cause the deaths of the sons of Bethlehem. Cox noted ironically, although Christians often say of Jesus, "He died for us," in this case, those children died for him.

Another student asked the distinguished theologian if he thought Jesus suffered from what is now known as survivor guilt. Dr. Cox answered that maybe Jesus did know and maybe it contributed to his unusual and extraordinary capacity for sympathizing with the suffering of others.

So, Joseph obeys the angel, gets up, and takes his wife and newborn son on the long dangerous journey through the savage wasteland of the Sinai desert. In so doing he and his family are refugees. Jesus the child is Jesus the refugee: fleeing to find refuge in the country where his Jewish ancestors had been oppressed millennia before.

We see immediately the parallels between this story and several in the Hebrew Scriptures. This is a recurring narrative of faithful people leaving the Promised Land and traveling to Egypt:

1. Abram and Sarai settle in Canaan, but in a famine retreat to Egypt for food (Genesis 12).
2. When the sons of Jacob face starvation, they travel to Egypt, the Breadbasket of the Near East, where they find both food and, much to their chagrin, their brother Joseph whom they had sold into slavery (Genesis 42-50).
3. Then there is the unmistakable parallel between Moses and Jesus. In Exodus 1 Pharaoh is killing Hebrew male infants, and in Matthew 1 Herod is committing the same heinous, hideous crime. Both Moses and Jesus are rescued by the obedience of family members to divine directives.

4. There is, of course, the severely painful parallel that as God delivered God's people from Egypt with the tragic deaths of the firstborn of Egypt, so now God's rescue of the Holy Family involved tragic consequences to the youngest children of Bethlehem.

How in the world did Joseph, Mary, and young Jesus survive as refugees in Egypt? Non-biblical tradition suggests that they used the gifts of gold, frankincense, and myrrh given to them by the Magi to survive in a foreign land. Those universally valued gifts could have provided food, housing, and diapers for a good long time.

While in Egypt, Joseph has a second dream in which God speaks to him. He is again told by an angel, "Get up and take your wife and son home to Israel. Herod the terrorist is now dead" (Matthew 2: 19-20). Joseph does exactly what he is told to do. But when they get home, Joseph hears that Herod's son is now on the throne and he is afraid to go there. Then Joseph has a third dream in which he is advised to go to Galilee. He takes his family to settle in the town of Nazareth, fulfilling a First Testament prophecy in Hosea.

As we reflect on this unusual story unique to Matthew, we note several valuable insights and ask a couple critical questions:

First, we see a wonderful example of faith, trust, and obedience in Joseph. We have already been told earlier in chapter 1 that Joseph is a righteous man, that he wanted to call off his marriage to Mary without humiliating her because she was pregnant with somebody else's child. Now we see Joseph caring for his fiancé and the special child that has come to this teenage couple.

Joseph is a model of obedience as he is twice told in the text to get up and take his family with him. Twice he got up and did as told without question. "Get up" and "got up" are translated from the Greek verb *egerio,* the same word Matthew uses when he refers to the resurrection of Jesus, to his rising from the dead. The rescue of Jesus from death as a baby by his father's getting up and taking him to Egypt and then back home to Israel is a foreshadowing of Jesus getting up from the grave and rescuing us from death and taking us home with him to his Father's house.

Second, we see Jesus fulfills Israel's role, called by God out of Egypt. Jesus is the second Moses, the new Moses, the greater Moses. According to Matthew, Jesus fulfills the First Testament prophecies of the Messiah in the lineage of King David. Five of those prophetic passages are quoted in Matthew's first two chapters. Jesus is God's providentially favored child, God's very son.

Third, we see in this passage how Jesus himself became a refugee. It was not his choice. It was a matter of survival. His family was forced by brutal circumstances to flee their homeland and to migrate to a faraway place. As an infant, Jesus became an immigrant. Before he was Jesus of Nazareth, he was Jesus of Egypt. He, Mary, and Joseph were Palestinian refugees, as it were.

Maybe this story can touch our hearts and stretch our minds to sympathize more with the circumstances today that drive families to cross borders, with or without proper documentation, to survive or escape economic, political, or military oppression.

Do you remember a tragic story from the Mediterranean

Sea in late fall of 2013 that made world headlines? An overcrowded migrant boat sailing from Tripoli, Libya capsized one-half mile from an Italian island. Between 450 and 500 migrants from Africa seeking a better life were aboard. At least 114 died, including two pregnant women. Most did not know how to swim. The Associated Press article on October 5 of the "worst-ever Mediterranean refugee disaster" concluded with this sentence, "Italian officials demanded a comprehensive European Union immigration policy to deal with the tens of thousands of migrants fleeing poverty and strife in Africa and the Middle East."

Jesus was a refugee. His family migrated from one land to another to save his life. Maybe his family's experience can make the nations of the world more sympathetic to and supportive of migrations necessitated by dire economic, political, or military circumstances to save one's life. If Jesus' family had not migrated, would Christianity have been born?

Fourth, this story leads me to ask: Where do we go for refuge? Where do we find a safe place, strength, and protection when the going gets tough in our lives? Sometimes the tough times touch each of us: our credit card is compromised, our job is eliminated, our marriage ends, our pet is put to sleep, our best friend receives a terminal diagnosis. The refugee to Egypt becomes our refuge, of course. Jesus says, "I will make my home with you. I will never fail you nor forsake you."

Fifth, we ask: For whom can we be a refuge? Who needs a port of peace in a stormy time of transition? How may we be sensitive to our neighbors, friends, family members, and fellow disciples who could use an encouraging word, a kind deed, or a special prayer? When I served communion to hundreds of folks at the annual 11:00 p.m. Christmas Eve service in Downtown Denver for twelve years, I estimate I did not know 95 percent of them. Probably 90 percent of them had no connection to the congregation other than at Christmas. But to that historic, holy house they came, a refuge which will continue to be a safe place for children of all ages in the name of Jesus, the refugee who found refuge in a foreign land.

Matthew wants us to know that at Jesus' birth, violent forces sought his life, just as they had the life of Moses. The violent forces at his birth foreshadow the violence that will eventually lead to his crucifixion.

Nevertheless, Jesus is delivered from Herod's maniacal, murderous intent, just as the people of God were delivered from Pharaoh. Even more so, Jesus will eventually be delivered from death itself. Matthew dares to see things as they are and still know that God is working, even in the worst we can do. The real joy of Christmas is this: Nothing can defeat the promise of Immanuel, God with us, the refugee who is our refuge today, tomorrow, and forever more.

Reflection Questions:

When have you sought refuge in your life?

How does this wisdom tale of Jesus as a refugee shape your Christology?

For whom can you be a refuge?

Where do you go for refuge?

CHAPTER NINE

Jesus and the Most Interesting Man in the World

Wisdom Text: Acts 2:22-24, 32-36

The most interesting man in the world, who is he? Who really is the most interesting man in the world? Several years ago, I asked our church staff that question as we approached Easter. They came back with a variety of candidates. Our office manager said Neil Armstrong. Do you remember him? He was the first man to walk on the moon. The year was 1969. He was completely humble about his signal accomplishment and chose to speak extraordinarily little about it, and to never profit from it. Our business administrator said her dad is the most interesting man in the world because he has more common sense than anyone in the world and can always make her laugh. Her second choice was Jimmy Buffett, a fun entertainer who, in her words, "has taken to a new level the success of doing what you love and getting paid for it." Our youth director said Thich Nhat Hanh, a Buddhist monk, author, poet, and peace activist who was exiled from Vietnam and who crosses national, political, spiritual, and religious borders to encourage peace in the world. Our communications director chose Mark Zuckerberg, the young billionaire founder of Facebook who has transformed the way the world communicates. The adult director called Sir Richard Branson the Most Interesting. He said the British business magnate is "a sort of well-funded cowboy, boldly riding his imagination into places no one previously could have imagined or afforded to go."

The world is certainly full of interesting men. British composer, philanthropist, activist, and entertainer Sir Elton John recently turned 73. He is a colorful character. Country singer Willie Nelson is 87 and should make any interesting man list.

Maybe the most interesting person in the world is not a man at all. Maybe her name is a solo one: Madonna or Gaga or Beyoncé or Oprah or Kate, the Duchess of Cambridge. Or maybe her name is Mary - the original Madonna, not the Material Girl - but the spiritual girl, the unmarried, pregnant teenager who said to her Heavenly Father, "Let it be to me according to your word" (Luke 1:38).

To discover who the Most Interesting Man really is we turn to that resource which has influenced lives for many years, and which is found in many homes around the world. Many of our homes have more than one. You can find one in every hotel and motel room. I am talking not about the Bible just yet, but about the television. You can find him on the TV: network, cable, and satellite stations alike. There he is – daring, dashing, debonair – the TV voice-over declaring, "He IS the most interesting man in the world." You have probably seen one or more of the numerous commercials for a brand of beverage that shows the 70+ year-old actor named Jonathan Goldsmith doing a series of extraordinary feats which define him as the most unique human being on planet earth.

And while the suave, sophisticated, self-confident man is doing his thing, the voice-over tells us all about the most interesting man in the world.

- People hang on his every word, even the prepositions.
- His reputation precedes him like lightning precedes thunder.
- When in Rome, they do as he does.
- When he pats you on the back, you put it on your resume.
- His pillows are cool on both sides.
- He speaks fluent French, in Russian.
- He lives vicariously through himself.
- He once had an awkward moment just to see how it feels.
- His mother has a tattoo that reads "Son."
- His personality is so magnetic, he is unable to carry credit cards.

You and I may find amusing the advertising concept of the commercial, but guess what? Since the ad campaign ran from 2006-20018, sales of the product in the U.S. increased over 22 percent while sales of other foreign beverages in the U.S. have fallen four percent. And if you do not think these commercials are impacting perhaps unintended target audiences, listen to this. The actor, Jonathan Goldsmith, was in a restaurant recently. A man went up to him and told the actor that he had asked his young son what he wanted to be when he grew up. The boy replied, "I want to be the most interesting man in the world." Perhaps, unconsciously, or not, all of us would like to be as suave, sophisticated, and self-confident as the man in the beverage commercial. Who would not want to be as daring, debonair, and dashing as he? But is he REALLY the most interesting man in the world? I do not think so.

No, the most interesting man in the world is not a fictional character in a series of popular 21st century 30-second television beverage commercials. No, he is a first-century historical individual whose story is chronicled in the world's all-time best-selling book. In fact, he is the central character of this narrative that has sold over 1.5 billion copies in 2,400 languages and dialects in the past 600 years. His name is Jesus, and he is the most interesting man in the world.

In the wisdom tale, Peter calls Jesus of Nazareth first "a man" and then "this man." What does the three-times denying fisherman Peter have to say about "this man" that would make him the most interesting man in the world?

Peter proclaims Jesus "a man attested by God with deeds of power, wonder and signs that God did through him ..." (Acts 2:22). Peter goes on to proclaim about this man "that he was crucified and killed by the hands of those outside the law ...." Then Peter declares the decisive, definitive, death-defying deed of the Divine. He says of Jesus in verse 24, "But God raised him up, having freed him from death, because it was impossible for him to be held in its power." Stronger than death. Talk about interesting.

Peter does not stop there. He proceeds to poetically proclaim that "this Jesus whom God raised up has been exalted at the right hand of God ... and that God has made him both Lord and Messiah." Talk about an interesting man. Lord and Messiah are ultimate titles. Lord means God. It means Master. Jesus even has a golf tournament on Easter named after him: The Masters, of course.

Later in the book of Revelation, Jesus is crowned as "the King of kings and the Lord of lords" (Revelation 17:14). These words are most often heard from Handel's Messiah at the closing choral coronation of Easter services. Can anyone top "the King of kings and the Lord of lords"? Elvis Presley was the King of Rock and Roll. Michael Jackson was the King of Pop. Barry Bonds was the Home Run King. Those were all remarkably interesting men, but can they compare to the King who conquered death on Easter Sunday morning? I think not.

Why is Jesus Christ the most interesting man in the world? Simply put, Jesus transforms lives. His life is full of encounters in which those who met him experienced transformation. They were changed. They were healed. They were saved.

- The blind were made to see.
- The lame were made to walk.
- The deaf were made to hear.

These miracles all represent the life-changing power of Jesus in forgiving sin, removing guilt, and restoring hope. Persons who met Jesus were resurrected in spirit, born anew, and raised from the deaths of helplessness and hopelessness.

Why is Jesus the most interesting man in the world? **Because he welcomes all.** In unprecedented behavior for his day, he blessed babies, welcomed children, taught women, ate with sinners, touched lepers, hung out with tax collectors and prostitutes, healed foreigners, fed the hungry, and had compassion for the least, the last, and the lost. If that is not interesting, what is?

Why is Jesus the most interesting man in the world? **Because he turns the world upside down.** He makes the first, last, and the last, first. He humbles the exalted and exalts the humble. He tells the Roman governor, "You have no power." He says of children, "To such little ones as these belongs the reign of God." Jesus is compelling when he teaches, "Whoever loses her life will find it – and whoever keeps his life will end up losing it."

Why is Jesus the most interesting man in the world? **Because he takes just 12 guys – some fisherman, an IRS agent, a CPA, a physician, a couple of brothers, a zealot or two – and begins a movement that today numbers over two billion souls on all seven continents of planet earth who follow in his way.** All over the world there are schools, colleges, hospitals, clinics, mission stations, churches, chapels, and cathedrals built by the followers of Jesus who himself was a healer, a teacher, and a holy man of God.

Why is Jesus the most interesting man in the world? **Because he was holy and human.** Yes, he is called King and Lord and Master and Son of God, but he was also called the Son of Man. Read the stories of Jesus. His humanity is on full display. He wept, he slept, he was angry, he fasted a perfect 40 days, he was hungry, he was thirsty, he felt pity and compassion. Jesus was rejected, falsely accused, beaten, spat upon, mocked, humiliated, and hung on a cross to die.

Why is Jesus the most interesting man in the world? **Because he had a special heart for the hurting.** He affirmed our tears with his beatitude, "Blessed are those who mourn" (Matthew 5:4). He cried with sisters Mary and Martha at the death of their brother and his friend Lazarus. Jesus said to that grieving family and says to our families when death comes our way, "I am the resurrection and the life. Those who believe in me, even though they die, yet shall they live. I go to prepare a place for you. I will come again and take you to myself. Do not let your hearts be troubled. Do not let them be afraid" (John 11:25).

On the last day of his life, Jesus was presented by Pontius Pilate to the Passover crowd in Jerusalem. Pilate asked the people, "What shall I do with this Jesus who is called the Messiah?" The crowd cried, "Let him be crucified."

The question is "What will you do with the most interesting man in the world?" The Roman governor handed him over to the crowd to be crucified. At the cross, a Roman soldier said of the crucified king, "Truly this man was the Son of God." (Matthew 27:54). Will you crucify him as a criminal in your heart, or crown him as a King, as God's Son to rule over your life?

Let me tell you, Jesus is not only the most interesting man in the world, he is also the Most IMPORTANT Man in the World. He can transform your life. He can turn your world upside down, inside-out or right-side up. He can welcome you into his family. He can share your hurts and heal your heart. What will you do with the most interesting and important man in the world? You can join his family, pray for his cause, support his ministry, serve his world, learn his way, take up his cross, eat at his table, receive his grace, witness to his power, and sing his song.

Like that little boy who was so taken by the suave, sophisticated, self-confident actor he saw in the beverage commercial that he told his father that when he grew up, "I want to be the most interesting man in the world," so may we be taken by the self-giving Savior and Son of God that we can say to our Heavenly Father, "I want to be like the most interesting and important man in the world: Jesus Christ. I want to take his name: Christian. I want to walk in his footsteps."

At the end of every most interesting man in the world

beverage commercial, the most interesting man spoke this command to the viewers, "Stay thirsty, my friends." most interesting man in the world says to each of us, "When you drink, drink the Living Water." He says, in fact, "I am the Living Water. Drink from me. Let anyone who is thirsty come to me and let the one who believes in me drink."

Are you thirsty for that life-giving water of love, hope, joy, and peace? Are you thirsty for a new beginning, for deep significance, and a closer relationship with the most interesting and IMPORTANT man in the world? The great news is that Jesus Christ got up from a grave to give you and me all of these good things and more. Hallelujah. Hallelujah. Hallelujah.

Reflection Questions:

What was the intrigue which made the Most Interesting Man in the World commercials so successful? (Google them for a refresher, if needed.)

Other than Jesus, who do you think is the most interesting man in the world?

How thirsty are you for the Living Water?

And yes, who is the Most Interesting Woman in the world today? In history?

CHAPTER TEN

Jesus and Football

Wisdom Text: 1 Corinthians 9:24-27

The year is 1972. The month is January. The place is New Orleans. Super Bowl VI is about to be played. A few days before the championship contest, a reporter asks Dallas Cowboy star running back Duane Thomas about playing in the ultimate contest. The reflective running back responds, "If it's the ultimate game, how come they're playing it again next year?"

The National Football League Super Bowl Championship game has been played for over a half-century. The "ultimate game" in professional football is played annually and we may wonder, "What is all the fuss about a game?" No fuss really, but the fact is over 100 million persons will view the game, if for nothing else, the creative commercials for which advertisers are paying up to $4 million a 30-second spot. The fact is the Super Bowl is an economic stimulus package for the country.

From a spirituality standpoint, we acknowledge the ugly underbelly of the Super Bowl extravaganza, that of its being the largest human trafficking event of the year. Pimps transport women and children against their will to the city where the game is played, not for the biggest weekend in football, but for the largest weekend in prostitution in the United States.

Idolatry, gluttony, and inebriation are other less-than-healthy human behaviors that manifest across the land on this highest holy day of America's Athletic Industrial Complex. Police prepare for overzealous post-game celebrations. Super Bowl Sunday is the second-largest day of food consumption in the United States. Only on Thanksgiving Day do we eat more. Large amounts of alcohol are consumed during the Super Bowl. Police departments have noted a dramatic increase in calls on Super Bowl Sunday.

Players, coaches, and teams are idolized. Individuals and communities almost over-identify with their local heroes. After a city's team wins, its residents may well shout, "WE won." and citizens of the non-winning team may cry, "WE lost." Before anyone gets too emotionally invested in the success brought by a win in the ultimate game, I recall two professional football head coaches in Dallas and Denver whose teams both won two Super Bowls and each coach was later fired by his team. Why? Because they did not win enough. We are part of a culture which glorifies winning. We watch to see who will win the Golden Globe, the Oscar, the Emmy, the Grammy, or the Olympic Gold Medal. It is sad to hear some silly announcers say disparagingly of one of the 2,500 athletes at the Olympics, "He or she had to settle for the Silver Medal," as if finishing second best in the world is a failure.

There is another downside to football in particular, from Pop Warner to professional level, and that is the violence in the game. There is a penalty for unnecessary roughness, which implies that roughness in football is necessary. Sadly, players at all levels experience concussions, which over time can result in CTE – chronic traumatic encephalopathy – which leads to dementia, depression, memory loss, and, in some cases, to suicide or other premature deaths. Wise parents have to weigh the inherent risks, roughness, and the remote chance of their sons becoming the next Tom Brady or Peyton Manning before lining up to sign up their children, some as young as five years-old, to play pee-wee football.

So what can we say good about the Super Bowl game and about sports in general? Having noted some cultural deficiencies associated with our national passion, let us celebrate some positive values connected to athletic competition. These dimensions come straight from the wisdom tale. Did you know that sports are in the Bible? In this tale Paul employs athletic images to encourage his readers as they live in the larger game of life as members of Team Jesus. The apostle refers to running and boxing to teach four valuable lessons about how to truly succeed in life.

First, look at verse 24, "Do you not know that in a race the runners all compete, but only one receives the prize? Run in such a way that you may win it." In other words, DO YOUR BEST. Give it your supreme shot. Try your hardest in whatever endeavor or work or ministry you are in. Do not be content with mediocrity. It does not really matter if you come out on top or not: "only one receives the prize." What matters is your effort.

Did you know that over 50 percent of the 90 nations competing in the quadrennial Olympic Games are not going to win a single medal? Not even one. Did you know that over 80 percent of the over 2,500 athletes will not place in their events? They will not go home with a medal, a prize of any kind. Only one athlete can win the gold medal in each event.

Almost 90 years ago at the Summer Olympic Games in Los Angeles, a 21-year-old Texas woman named Babe Didrikson won two gold medals and a silver one in the 1932 track and field events. She later became a phenomenally successful professional golfer, winning 82 tournaments, including a record 17 in a row. Six times she was chosen "Female Athlete of the Year," and in 1950 was voted by the Associated Press as "The World's Greatest Female Athlete of the First-Half of the 20th Century." Babe Didrikson Zaharias died of cancer in 1956 at the age of 45.

When I was a boy growing up in Beaumont, Texas, I would ride my bicycle to the Forest Lawn Cemetery. It is now the resting place of my mother, father, and sister. But as a child I went to see the grave of Babe. On her tombstone is no mention of her unsurpassed athletic accomplishments. Just her name, dates of birth and death, and these words, "It's not whether you won or lost, but how you played the game."

It should not be so important to us that we come out on top, that we are the best in life. What should be most important is that we try our best, give our best in whatever venture, job, challenge, or ministry that comes to us or we choose. Whether it is teaching school, being a student, or playing in the Super Bowl, do your best. "Run in such a way that you may obtain the prize," Paul says.

A second sports truth we learn from Paul is in verse 25. The Apostle writes there, "Athletes exercise self-control in all things". The message is this: SELF-CONTROL is required for success in athletics, and also in the game of life. Self-control involves discipline, moderation, training, and fitness. Sometimes you may hear a sports announcer remark that a certain basketball player is "playing out of control." That is never a compliment and means the player is undisciplined. If a downhill skier gets out of control, it could be dangerous, even life threatening. Two dozen years ago I conducted a memorial service for a friend and member of a Texas church I previously pastored. Richard died in Colorado two weeks earlier from injuries sustained in a collision with a tree while snow-skiing. Each year, dozens of skiers sustain serious or fatal injuries from losing control.

It is a basic lesson of life that we need control and discipline in our lives. There are no successful athletes, singers, performers, or Christians who do not exercise self-control. Three of the most important words that we can ever learn to say are "No, thank you." All of us need to learn to say and think positively, "My body is a gift from God. It is God's temple. I refuse to abuse my body with excessive food, drink, drugs, or with any illicit or immoral relationship in the eyes of God." If we drive fast, live fast, or spend fast, we may bring damage to ourselves or others by being out of control. "Athletes exercise control in all things," says Paul. The final fruit of the Holy Spirit he lists in Galatians 5 is "self-control"; a self-directed discipline to the glory of God. So, let every member of Team Jesus exercise such self-control in all things.

A third sports lesson in the text is LIVING WITH PURPOSE. In verse 26, Paul declares, "So I do not run aimlessly, nor do I box as though beating the air." In other words, "I run with a purpose – I compete with a goal in mind." It seems many persons today are going through life without a purpose. They are running aimlessly. In 2002, a California pastor wrote a book that has become the best-selling hardback book in English of all time with 50 million copies. Next to the Bible, it is the most translated book in history, now in over 80 languages. The phenomenal success of Rick Warren's *The Purpose-Driven Life* testifies to the hunger of people to travel with a direction in life, to live life on purpose. Every mental health professional will tell you we all need a purpose, a core cause, a reason to get up in the morning, a motivation that drives us to hope and dream beyond ourselves and our needs and lives.

What is your purpose in life? What on earth are you here for? Warren says we were made by God, for God:

- Planned for God's pleasure.
- Formed for God's family.
- Created to become like Christ.
- Shaped for serving God.
- Made for a mission.

Our bottom-line purpose is to love God with our heads, hearts, and hands, and our neighbor as ourselves. "So I do not run aimlessly, nor do I box as though beating the air," Paul declared. And neither should we be without a purpose as we travel life's way.

The final way we can live with an athletic faith is the by the example we set. Look at verse 27. Paul confesses there, "But I punish my body and enslave it, so that after proclaiming to others, I myself should not be disqualified". Isn't that an amazing statement by the Apostle? He was so concerned about being an example to others. He wanted to make sure that he practiced what he preached, that he walked his talk. He did not want to appear to be hypocritical or deceitful. He did not want others to say, "Look at old Paul. He says one thing but does another."

Friends, for better or for worse, you and I are examples. We are models. We influence people every day by the way we live, the choices we make, the things we say, the way we spend our time and money, the things we do or do not do. Our Lord said, "Let your light so shine before others that they may see your good works and give glory to your Father who is in heaven" (Matthew 5:16).

In January 2014, I was in a hotel ballroom listening to Governor John Hickenlooper deliver the "State of the State" address to hundreds of members of Denver area Rotary Clubs. The governor, himself a Rotarian, shared with us a story I had never heard. He said that in July 2012, he went to the hospitals following the Aurora Theatre shooting to visit victims and their families. It is impossible to forget difficult, dark days in our community, state, and nation.

Then Governor Hickenlooper said, "In every hospital room I entered, either a patient or a family member was excited to tell me that Denver Bronco Quarterback Peyton Manning had called to express his concern, support, and prayers for the survivors and their family."

Peyton Manning did that before he ever threw a pass in a game for the Broncos. He did not tell the press. It was not about him. He was simply putting his faith into action as a disciple of Jesus. We do not worship Peyton Manning or any other player or Super Bowl Champion. But we do rejoice in the good role model he and other athletes are by contributing to the common good through their generosity, compassion, and sacrifice. We, too, are called as athletes are, to:

- Do our best.
- Exercise self-control.
- Run with a purpose.
- Be a positive example to others as followers of Jesus Christ.

The inspiration and motivation for our doing so comes not from winning ribbons, trophies, or medals. Rather it comes from an inner assurance and faith expressed by the anonymous author of Hebrews who advises us in these athletic terms: "Let us run with perseverance the race that is set before us, looking to Jesus the pioneer and perfecter of our faith, who for the sake of the joy that was set before him endured the cross, disregarding its shame, and has taken his seat at the right hand of the throne of God" (Hebrews 12: 1-2,).

Reflection Questions:

Were you aware of the Super Bowl's underbelly?

How did it make you feel?

Does the violence of some sports disturb you?

What sports do you enjoy and why?

What lessons did you learn in physical education or sports competition?

What kind of example are you in self-control?

Do you think Jesus played Spin the Dreidel or hopscotch?

CHAPTER ELEVEN

Jesus and Christopher Columbus

Wisdom Text: 2 Corinthians 5:1, 16-21

"In fourteen hundred ninety-two Columbus sailed the ocean blue." Do you remember the verse from childhood? I was taught the Italian explorer was a hero, the discoverer of America. Over 50 U.S. cities are named after him, as well as a prominent district and university. October 12, 1992 marked the 500th anniversary of Columbus' arrival in a world new to Europe. The half-millennium was marked with festivities all weekend. At the Rice University-Southern Methodist University football game on October 10 in Houston, my son and I saw and heard a band with 500 instruments. Our ears rang for days. On Friday of that week, a new movie about Columbus hit the theaters across America.

Yet not all the Columbus events that weekend over 25 years ago were celebrations. Some were commemorations not of a joyful discovery, but of a destructive invasion. It almost goes without saying, of course, that Christopher Columbus did not "discover" America. It was already here, inhabited by human beings already present for thousands of years. What he did was put America on the map for Europe. He did not realize the significance of his supposed discovery. Columbus went to his grave still believing that he had found a short cut to India.

A non-glossed reading of history paints a far less flattering picture of Columbus than a heroic mariner. His goal was gold. He captured, tortured, and killed native American men, women, and children who resisted his greedy ambitions. Even though he was later imprisoned and died penniless, he insisted on being addressed as Admiral, a title bestowed by Ferdinand and Isabella after he returned from his first voyage.

I do not know how you view Christopher Columbus or mark each October 12 over five centuries since he first set foot in the New World: a great hero, a harbinger of death, or most likely somewhere in between. As I have read about and studied his life over my adult years, I do know there are admirable qualities about this explorer which are relevant and exemplary for God's people in any season.

First, Christopher Columbus was persistent. As a foreigner, he struggled to get an audience with Queen Isabella and King Ferdinand of Spain. When he finally had the chance to make his request for ships, supplies, and funding, the queen appointed a committee to study the proposal. The committee met for five years. They concluded, "This idea is impossible." Columbus persisted. The second committee was formed and met for another year. They concluded, "The trip is too expensive." Only after his third request did Columbus get a green light from the queen to sail. The lesson here is clear. When we are faced with resistance, we need persistence. We need to see the obstacles as opportunities to be creative and discover ways to go over, around, or through them.

We may need to be persistent in our patience when meeting resistance. Columbus's plan to reach the east by sailing west would have been unfulfilled had he not been patient in his efforts to gain funding for the project. Parents need persistence in dealing with resistant children. Politicians need persistence in dealing with problems without overnight solutions. Voters need persistence in dealing with resistant politicians. Whenever you meet resistance, employ persistence.

A second quality in Christopher Columbus was his courage. When he and those other 86 sailors weighed anchor and departed Spain down the Tinto River Friday, August 12, 1492, they did not know what the future held for them. They may never return, never see loved ones. It took Columbus months to recruit a crew willing to risk life and limb on an enterprise to seek new routes. There were those who believed they might sail off the face of the earth and never see their families again. There is something biblical about stepping out in faith and courage as Columbus did. One day Jesus called Peter to step out of the boat in faith and walk on the water in faith. There are times when we must act with similar courage, when like Columbus, we must be willing to raise our sails and set off in into uncharted and uncomfortable waters.

This leads to the third admirable quality Columbus possessed, faith in God. He was a devout Christian, a pious man who saw himself as a messenger of God in his plan to sail to faraway places. Any riches he discovered would be used to rid the Holy Land of the infidels who had conquered it. All of the explorer's journals were replete with faith, prayers, devotions, and biblical images. His very name means "Christ bearer." The first thing Columbus did upon reaching shore on San Salvador on October 12, 1492 was to kneel and pray. He saw himself as a servant of Christ. Though a man of his time who enslaved the natives he encountered, he always saw himself as a servant of God and sought guidance for his life and mission. It is easy to forget in this busy world that our primary identity comes not from what we have, where we live, or to whom we are related. Our single most important mark of identification is that of being God's precious children. We need not quote scripture frequently as Columbus did to be holy.

Call Columbus an invader or a discoverer, a hero or a harbinger of death, a servant of God or gold, he was probably all of these to some degree across the years. He did open the doors to a new era in human history. He did discover terra nova, a new world. He brought exploration, expansion, and exploitation. As we think of the footprint of Columbus on world history, we must think of another single man who impacted human history, who brought a new world order, and "turned the world upside down."

This man's name was Jesus Christ. Paul says in the wisdom source, "If anyone is in Christ, that person is a new creation; the old is gone and the new is come" (2 Corinthians 5:17). In other words, Christ brings us into a new world. To be "in Christ" is to discover Christ, to belong to Christ, and to discover several significant things.

First, it means a new way of looking at things. Paul says we no longer see anyone else from a worldly point of view, but from the point of reconciled relationships. Relationships are the key to this new world in Christ: not things, not money, but people in healthy relationships of peace and harmony with God and one another. Christianity is not a religion, but a relationship with Christ which affects all other relationships we have.

Second, the good news about this new world of reconciled relationships God gives us in Christ is that it is available to all. The apostle affirms, "If anyone be in

Christ ...." Anyone includes an invitation to everyone. God has entrusted this message, one of reconciliation, for us to share with others. God is working through us to reach others. No one is excluded. All are welcome. As with Holy Communion, the invitation is to all. No one is excluded.

Third, God in Christ promises us a new world in an ultimate way. God declares that in the resurrection of Christ his followers share in the mystery of victory over death. One January Saturday in 2004, I stood to lead three different families in a trio of services of worship of God in thanksgiving for the lives of their precious loved ones. That is a lot of grief and pain to absorb. In one of our affirmations of faith, we profess, "I believe in the life of the world to come." Paul proclaims in 2 Corinthians 5, "For we know that if the earthly tent we live in is destroyed, we have a building, a house not made with hands, eternal in the heavens."

Very, very few people have an opportunity such as the persistent, faithful, and courageous Christopher Columbus to discover or put on the map a new world as he did. But along the way in life we discover the wonder and magic of many new worlds: of reading, music, education, friends, travel, food, grandchildren, and retirement. But the most important discovery we will ever make is that of a new world in Christ, becoming a new person who sees things differently, who enjoys reconciled relationships and who looks forward to the final frontier of a new world of eternal life God has prepared for all who love God.

Reflection Questions:

What did you learn about Christopher Columbus in school?

What did you learn about Columbus in this wisdom tale?

Was Columbus a hero, zero, or a bit of both?

How does the persistence, courage, and faith in the God of Columbus encourage you?

What are you yet anxious to discover?

How are you like Columbus?

Christopher means "Christ-bearer." How do you bear witness to Jesus Christ?

CHAPTER TWELVE

Jesus and Willie Nelson

Wisdom Text: Ecclesiastes 3:1-13

The baby boy arrived on the last day of April 1933. He was born in the small central Texas town of Abbot to Ira and Myrtle. William grew up in the Methodist Church there and learned to sing some of the great hymns of faith: *Amazing Grace, Will the Circle Be Unbroken* and *Just as I Am.* The message of these songs stuck with him as he traveled life's journey with all of its twists and turns. William loved the Methodist Church, and as an adult served on the board of one of its seminaries. In recent years, he has helped raise significant funds for the global mission work of The United Methodist Church.

The wisdom text is about time, about approaching a new year, a new age, a new season of life. This transition time in our lives declares that human beings are "to be happy and to enjoy themselves as long as they live" and that "God's gift is that all should eat and drink and take pleasure in all their toil." We turn to the 87-year-old native Texan named William as a model for how to have a great time in whatever season you are living.

You probably know William better by his nickname, "Willie" Nelson. He has been a member of the Country Music Hall of Fame since 1993. In 1998, he was honored by the Kennedy Center in Washington, D.C. In the year 2000,

Nelson was presented a Grammy Lifetime Achievement Award. You may or may not like Mr. Nelson's music, hairstyle, politics, or attire, but there are some things in his life which are exemplary in terms of living life fully, joyfully, and meaningfully as a friend and follower of Jesus. There are six short and significant lessons we gain from walking with Willie for a while.

The first lesson we learn from Willie Nelson and the scripture is this: Stay busy. This text talks twice about human toil and "the business God has given everyone to be busy with." A good part of a good life starts with being active and productive. How does Mr. Nelson stay active? As he approaches his 88th birthday, he continues to record albums and play multiple concerts a year. He is on the road again and again and again. He has recorded 200 albums over six decades.

Staying active is good for our bodies and our minds and souls. Staying busy is much more than laboring in our jobs. It means caring for ourselves, as well. The Franklin Covey group recently released the results of its annual survey of the Top 10 New Year's Resolutions among over 15,000 Americans. They include: get out of debt, save money, quit smoking, lose weight, exercise more, get organized, work less, and play more.

Obviously, those are interrelated at several levels and none will be accomplished without hard work, without staying quite busy. Yes, there is a time for regular rest in our lives, but you and I will be better people as we stay active, productive, and work hard in our personal lives.

A second connected new year lesson from Willie Nelson: Maintain balance. Along with work and being busy, there is a needed time to play. In addition to singing, Mr. Nelson has another profound passion. He enjoys whacking at a little white ball and chasing it around a course until that balls falls in 18 holes in the ground after as few whacks as possible. Nelson's recording studio is located next to a golf course. When asked about his retirement plans, Willie says, "All I do is play music and golf – which one do you want me to give up?"

No one should work all of the time, and no one should play all of the time, either. We all need a balance in our lives. That is what the wisdom text is about: having times "for planting and harvesting, breaking down and building up, weeping and laughing, mourning and dancing, being together and being apart, seeking and letting go, speaking and being silent, working and playing." Fully alive people are multidimensional people. They have more to their lives than just work or just play or just one activity or passion. They maintain a healthy balance.

A third valuable lesson that we learn from Mr. Nelson to help us have a great new year is this: Use your Jesus-given gifts. When asked to explain his seeming inexhaustibility, this popular and prolific singer says, "If you don't use your voice, you lose it." The Bible teaches us that we all have gifts from God. Life itself and work are good gifts from God we learn in the text. Beyond that, some of us have talents and spiritual gifts of music, leadership, generosity, compassion, teaching, helping, and encouragement to use in our lives.

Willie Nelson is right: we use our gifts, or we risk losing them. If someone cared enough to give you a gift at Christmas or on your birthday, he or she did not intend for you to leave that gift in the box or put it on a shelf in the closet. That giver wants you to employ and enjoy that gift. Likewise, God bequeaths us with gifts not to be hidden under bushel baskets, but to be employed and enjoyed. We will abound as we use our gifts from Jesus.

Which leads to lesson #4 to be to Jesus people: Live for others. Something tells me that Willie Nelson may not be in worship every Sunday. Nor are many of us. However, for over 30 years now, Mr. Nelson has organized, recruited other musicians, and played himself at the annual Farm Aid concerts across the country. His efforts since 1985 have benefited countless folks not only with millions of dollars but with the priceless gifts of hope, compassion, and encouragement. In April 2020, Willie did a virtual concert raising $500,000 for Farm Aid.

Do you want to be a healthy, whole follower of Jesus? Live for others. Use your gifts for others. Share your time, your talent, your treasure with those in need. There is no greater reward than a life which is focused on others and doing what one can to benefit them. Giving to others is the rent we pay for life on this earth. In December 2007, the Rocky Mountain News reported that a country singer donated $40,000 to the city of Vancouver, Washington, its Humane Society, and Boys and Girls Club.

The donor was named Willie Nelson. He gave back to this city in gratitude for the fact that those folks there bought some of his first records over 60 years ago. He wanted to thank them for their help. Who are you grateful to and what are you grateful for? You and I will move from good to great as we live for others, sharing our time and treasure.

A fifth lesson for a fulfilling life we have already touched on from Mr. Nelson's life is this: Enjoy what you do. Have you ever seen Willie Nelson sing in a live concert or on television? In February of 2006, our family saw him perform with David Allen Coe at the Oil Palace in Tyler, Texas. We were not far from the stage on that cold Saturday night with 7,500 other folks, fans, and friends of the country music legend. We could see the pleasure this performer took in his work. He obviously enjoyed playing his old, beat-up guitar named Trigger, and sharing such contradictory wisdom as "Mama, Don't Let Your Babies Grow Up to be Cowboys" and "My Heroes Have Always Been Cowboys."

Again, God's word says to us in Ecclesiastes 3:13 that we are to "take pleasure in all of our toil." You and I will never have a fulfilling life unless we enjoy what we are doing. If we are not enjoying it, we need to do something new or get a new attitude. If you have a staff of 30 people in your office or company, probably three of them need to move on to something else. Take pleasure in all your toil: housework, yard work, volunteer work, homework, and as well as work-work.

Now last, and maybe most important of all to be a vital disciple of Jesus: Recognize your mortality. Willie Nelson says, "While I've still got the time, I want to play with as many of the musicians I love as possible." The talented Texas troubadour is in touch with reality. He knows his days are limited and that there will come a day he will no longer be able to make music in this world.

Do you believe that one day you will die? Remember the wisdom text. First on the list, "For everything there is a season ... a time to be born, and a time to die." The death rate is still 100 percent. Though denial is extraordinarily strong, and the younger we are the more likely we are to believe we can cheat death, the reality is no one gets out of this world alive.

We cannot truly live until we come to terms that one day our life on earth will be over. Such is the reminder of the wisdom writer in the key verse 12 of the text, where he declares of human beings, "I know that there is nothing better for them than to be happy and to enjoy themselves as long as they live."

On the final Sunday of 2004 at noon, just about the time he had pronounced the benediction for over 40 years as a Methodist pastor, Dr. Bill Hinson closed his eyes in death, four weeks after suffering a debilitating stroke at age 68. Bill was the senior pastor of the First UMC in Houston from 1983-2001, an author, and a popular preacher across the continent. I had Bill as a guest preacher in several of my churches. He was a friend to many across the United Methodist connection. Bill often said, "When I die, I hope I can say I was used up for the Lord."

There is a blessed mystery about this gift called life. But there is also a holy reality in this temporary time here and it is this: God is good, and God can be trusted, come what may in the eternal future. As we move forward in an anxious season of an extended pandemic, individually and as the Body of Christ, we do so by following the example of our Methodist brother Willie Nelson and his friend Jesus by:

- Staying busy
- Maintaining balance
- Using our gifts
- Benefiting others

- Enjoying what we do
- Recognizing our mortality.

So that when our time of departure arrives, we may leave this world for our true home, in the absolute confidence and conviction as did Bill Hinson, that our lives have been fully "used up for the Lord."

Reflection Questions:

What 2-3 new things did you learn about Willie Nelson in this reflection?

What is your favorite Willie Nelson song?

Of the six lessons shared by Jesus and Willie, which 2-3 connect to your life most closely?

At age 87 Willie was still on the road in 2020, virtually making music with his friends to benefit Farm Aid during the Covid-19 pandemic. Is anyone surprised?

How can your life be ”all used up for the Lord” when the time of your departure arrives? (See 2 Timothy 4:6-8).

CHAPTER THIRTEEN

Jesus and Osama bin Laden

Wisdom Text: John 1:1-14

In December 2010, Supreme Leader Kim Jong Il of North Korea died of a heart attack at age 69. During his reign of 17 years, 2,000,000 of his subjects died of hunger. While the dictator spent billions of dollars amassing a nuclear arsenal, 10 percent of his subjects starved to death and another 154,000 citizens were arrested and held as political prisoners in large concentration camps across the country.

Two months before, Libyan dictator Muammar Gaddafi, who ruled his homeland for 42 years with an iron fist of military oppression, was killed by rebels in his hometown of Sirt. He, too, was 69.

Almost eight months before on a Sunday night, word spread across this country that Al-Qadea leader Osama bin Laden had been killed by a team of U.S. Navy Seals. Many of us remember where we were and what we felt when we heard the news that the one responsible for multiple mass-casualty attacks on civilian and military targets for almost two decades was now dead at age 54. The violent reign of terror of a combined 79 years by this unholy trinity of ruthless villains represents a painful period of destruction, death, and darkness almost unparalleled in human history.

As a result of the deaths of these three megalomaniacs, the planet seemed to be a little less dark, a little more light shone that December. As millions of Christians around the world light candles to welcome the light of the world each Holy Christmas season, we commemorate and, indeed, celebrate the truth of John's declaration of good news, "The light shines in the darkness, and the darkness did not overcome it" (John 1:5). The darkness of the world was personified in the life of one whose death was not unwelcomed by many on May 2, 2010. Osama bin Laden lived by the sword and died by the sword. The light of the world is personified in the life of the One whose birth we celebrate each December 25. Jesus of Nazareth brought light and life to all.

Osama and Jesus, darkness and light, death and life. They represent sharp contrasts, for sure, but also had several things in common when you stop and think about it:

- Both came from the Middle East.
- Both were rejected by their families.
- Both were highly motivated by their religious beliefs.
- Both had followers willing to die for them.
- Both were, indeed, willing to die for what they believed.

That is about where the similarities end. Osama and Jesus were vastly different in some significant ways:

- One was born in a cave – the other spent years hiding in a cave.
- One was born into a small, poor family – the other into a large, wealthy family.
- One's father was a poor carpenter – the other's was a billionaire construction magnate.

- One went about doing good – the other went about doing harm.
- One liberated women – the other oppressed women.
- One spoke the truth – the other misrepresented the truth.
- One sought to enhance life – the other sought to destroy life.
- One wept when he saw the city he loved about to have its buildings fall down – the other laughed when he saw the city he hated have its buildings fall down.
- One destroyed the World Trade Center – the other came to save the world and its people by trading his life for theirs and becoming the center of their lives.
- One became the most sought-after fugitive in the history of the world – the other is the most sought-after friend in the history of the world.
- One majored in hate and killing – the other majors in love and healing.
- One inspired fear – the other inspires faith.
- One sought to eliminate Christianity – the other is the center of Christianity.
- One was the son of Laden – the other is the Son of God.

Desperate, deluded, destructive dictators named Kim Jong, Muammar, and Osama bring their seasons of darkness on the stage of human history from time to time. The attack on America in 2001 orchestrated by Osama bin Laden drove us to the foundation of our faith – to seek God in prayer, in worship, in scripture, and in relationships with others. None of us born before 1990 will ever forget the assault on our senses and the sad, sober reminder each September 11 that we live in a fragile and fragmented world where the powers of darkness still rage in deadly and destructive ways.

The good news we are bold to proclaim each Christmas Eve is of a God who is not content to leave us or our world alone in its brokenness, darkness, and propensity for self-destruction. We need, welcome, and proclaim the message of the wisdom text, "The light shines in the darkness, and the darkness did not overcome it." And the message of an epistle, "For the grace of God has appeared, bringing salvation to all" (Titus 2:11).

On September 11, 2011, I had perhaps the most emotional and meaningful experience ever in 38 years as a pastor. It was my privilege to represent the Christian community in praying at the "Colorado Remembers 9-11" gathering in Civic Center Park, three blocks south of Trinity Church. The governor, the mayor, our two U.S. Senators, our Secretary of Interior, and 35,000 of our closest friends were there. I know not everyone came to hear the prayers of the four diverse clergy, nor to listen to the elected officials.

There was a music group 50 years-old which performed. Do you remember the group called the Beach Boys? I prayed there would be many "Good Vibrations" on that sunny Sunday afternoon in the park.

My "aha moment" from God came later that afternoon when I discovered that on the security bracelet, placed on my wrist when I arrived in the stage area, were two important alliterative words: "All Access." ALL ACCESS. That bracelet not only allowed me a seat on the stage to pray that day, but also granted me all the food I could eat, all the beverages I could drink, all the dignitaries I could invite to Denver's First Church, and access to a seat in the shade next to the stage to see and hear the Colorado Symphony and Colorado Children's Choir, both of which had Trinity Church members in their ranks. Those groups produced the music of heaven and angels that glorious day. I discovered, friends, that having "All Access" is an incredibly good thing, indeed.

The great news at Christmas is that in the birth, life, death, and resurrection of Jesus Christ, you, and I, and all in the world have been granted eternal access to God's riches in glory. That amazing, available, accessible, awesome light and love of God in the Christ Child is given freely to all who stumble in the darkness, brokenness, addictions, and humanness of this sometimes scary, yet beautiful, world. Thanks be to God for the light of Christ which shines in our world and in our hearts – a light that no darkness can overcome. That is the good news of God for the people of God. Thanks be to God.

Reflection Questions:

What do you recall about the death of Osama bin Laden in 2010?

What 2-3 comparisons between Osama and Jesus strike you as most significant?

What unlimited benefits does your faith plan provide access?

Can you name three Beach Boys number one hit songs?

What are your 2-3 favorite Christmas hymns?

CHAPTER FOURTEEN

Jesus and Contentment

Wisdom Text: Philippians 4:10-14

Richard Mouw is a philosopher and ethicist. He is the retired President of Fuller Theological Seminary in Pasadena, California. Several years ago, he was invited by some friends to attend a Rolling Stones concert at the Rose Bowl. They said they wanted to do some theological reflection on popular culture. There they were, this group of middle-age religious leaders at the Rolling Stones Voodoo Lounge Tour. They were calling their teenage children and holding up their cell phones so their kids could hear the Red Hot Chili Peppers warming up the crowd and know that their fathers were really there.

One of the pastors said to Dr. Mouw, "There are 85,000 people here. That is more than will be in all of the churches and synagogues of Pasadena this weekend. What would you say to them if you had the chance?" Mouw had no idea until Mick Jagger started singing the Stones' signature song, Satisfaction. Over 85,000 people began singing in unison, "I can't get no satisfaction, I can't get no satisfaction, 'Cause I try, and I try, and I try, and I try...."[5]

Folks in Pasadena, California, New York City, and around the globe can partake of great food, wield tremendous power,

5 R*olling Stones Voodoo Lounge Tour,* music and lyrics by Rolling Stones, Rose Bowl Stadium, Pasadena, October 19, 1994.

build grand mansions, engage in countless physical relationships, earn terminal degrees, and receive prestigious honors, but guess what? All of these turn out to be trivial pursuits. A hunger keeps resurfacing which cannot be satisfied with the material things of the world.

The Rolling Stones may have written and released the still popular song in 1965 – 55 years ago – but the frustration of a lack of satisfaction was articulated several millennia before in the First Testament book of Ecclesiastes. The wisdom writer voices the grim verdict that "All is vanity." The anonymous author may have been a little over the top, but he touched on a chronic condition of humankind: We are often dissatisfied, unhappy, depressed, discontented people.

We wrestle with the soul hunger for contentment and satisfaction in life. We take medicine, read bestsellers, listen to pop talk show counselors, join social groups, and buy unneeded material things to fill the hole of discontent in our homes and hearts. Sadly, it is not a winter or other season of discontent we experience, but a chronic disenchantment which gnaws at our inward being. We try and we try, and we try, and we try, but like the Rolling Stones, "we can't get no satisfaction." Mick Jagger and Keith Richards may have been grammatically challenged, but the British boys were theologically on target in their composition that in 2004 was named number two on the list of the 500 Greatest Songs of All Time by Rolling Stone magazine. Number one, of course, was Like a Rolling Stone by Bob Dylan.

How can we gain satisfaction in our lives? What is the source of true contentment? How can you and I be content in our lives in a time of profound political, economic, racial, and health turmoil in our nation and our world?

We are confronted, challenged, and comforted by a man of God named Paul. He used to be on a mission to destroy followers of Jesus and now he is one. Here is Paul writing to some fellow Christians. And he writes in the wisdom text, "I have learned to be content with whatever I have. I know what it is to have little, and I know what it is to have plenty. In any and all circumstances I have learned the secret of being well-fed and of going hungry, of having plenty and of being in need" (Phil. 4:12).

Where was Paul when he wrote these words? Yes, he was in Rome, but where in Rome? Was he staying at the Grand Rome Hyatt? Was he a guest of the Pope at the Vatican? No, Paul was in custody of the state. He was lodging in a Roman jail cell, awaiting news of whether or not he would be executed. You can go to Rome today and visit the prison of Peter and Paul. The apostle was lowered through a hole in the floor and dropped into a cavernous, damp pit. Paul was in the pits of prison when he penned the Philippian proclamation, "I have learned to be content with whatever I have."

What about us? Can we learn to be content within our circumstances, whatever they are? Adam Hamilton suggests four keys, which like the "secret" Paul referred to in this letter, can help us cultivate contentment in our lives.

First: Remember that it could be worse. Whatever pain or problem or person we are presently pressed by, it could be worse. One day Snoopy is lying on top of his doghouse, and he has a bitter spirit. It is Thanksgiving and Charlie Brown and his family are all inside having turkey and dressing and cranberry sauce while Snoopy is stuck on his doghouse with nothing but dog food. He is not at all happy about this until he is struck by this thought, "It could be worse. I could have been born a turkey."

Now, here is how you use this phrase, "It could be worse" to cultivate contentment.

The next time you get in your vehicle you are going to be tempted to think, "I would be content, if I have had a nicer, newer, more expensive vehicle." You are not going to do that. When you get into your vehicle, you are going to say, "It could be worse." With enormous passion and energy, you are going to say what? "It could be worse."

When you get home to wherever you live and walk through the door, you are going to be tempted to think, "If I just had a nicer, newer, bigger, better place, then I would be content." But instead of doing that, today when we walk through that door, we are going to say with great conviction, "It could be worse."

And then tomorrow morning, when you wake up and roll over, if you are married and see your spouse or partner, you are going to say... NO. Don't do that. This practice is an exercise in accentuating the positive, finding the silver lining, looking on the bright side in the constantly challenging circumstances of our lives. It reminds me of a proverb my father taught his children, "I was sad because I had no shoes, until I saw a man who had no feet." It can always be worse.

The second key to contentment is asking yourself a simple question, "How long will this make me happy?" Every day we are bombarded with billboard, Internet, newspaper, radio, TV, and telephone ads telling us we will be content, happy, and satisfied by purchasing a particular product. We are subtly seduced into retail therapy. We are given the message that the newer, flashier computer, car, or clothing item will change us for the better. There, for sure, is a moment of satisfaction when we make the purchase. But, as Adam Hamilton notes, "The happiness lasts as long as it takes to open the box."

Have you ever thought you simply had to have something and later found out it was not all it was cracked up to be? Many folks have closets, garages, and attics filled with items they could not live without. You do not have to raise your hand. Have you ever been to a church or community rummage sale?

A helpful question to ask before making a major purchase is, "How long will this make me happy?" As I was writing this wisdom tale offering one morning at home, the phone rang. It was an 800-number, and I chose to answer with the plan to ask the caller to put me on his no-call list. But before I could make that request, I heard this wonderful pitch for how only $2.50 a month for five months, I could upgrade my "grandfather" satellite TV package by adding all the premium movie channels AND the NFL ticket. Now, that was not fair for him to call the week that the National Football League season begins, was it? I was tempted. Oh, was I tempted. All the NFL games - all of them. All of the Dallas Cowboys games, even though I lived in Denver. Emotion almost trumped reason. But I do not watch most of the channels I have now. There is a sports saturation already on the available channels. Alas, I thanked the caller for his kind offer, because in reply to the question, "How long will this make me happy?" the honest answer was, "NFL – not for long."

The third key to contentment is to develop a grateful heart. Gratitude is essential to contentment. The apostle Paul, who had written to the Thessalonians, "Give thanks in all circumstances, for this is the will of God for you in Christ Jesus" (I Thess. 5:18), did just that in his letter from prison. He told the Philippians in the opening verses, "I thank my God every time I remember you...because of your sharing in the gospel from the first day until now."

A grateful heart focuses on what we have and not on what we may lack. A grateful heart recognizes that all of life is a gift. The anonymous writer to the Hebrews advised his readers, "Keep your life free from the love of money and be content with what you have" (Heb. 13:5). That sounds a lot like Paul in the wisdom text, "I have learned to be content with whatever I have." It also echoes his counsel to his young colleague Timothy in chapter 6 of his first letter to him, "There is great gain in godliness combined with contentment; for we brought nothing into the world, it is certain that we take nothing out of it; but if we have food and clothing, we will be content with these...for the love of money is the root of all kinds of evil" (1Timothy 6:6, 10).

In the midst of the fears and frets of life, we have much for which to be grateful: forgiveness, friends, freedom, family, and a faith fellowship. As an unthankful heart yields discontent and depression, so a grateful heart yields joy and contentment.

Fourth and finally: Ask yourself, "Where does my soul find true satisfaction?" The world answers by telling us that we find satisfaction in ease and comfort, in luxury, and affluence. The Bible, however, has a different answer. From Genesis to Revelation, the message is the same: We find our satisfaction in God alone. Our restless, hungry hearts are meant to seek after God and to find their home there. The Psalmist cried, "O God, you are my God. I seek you, my soul thirsts for you..." (Psalm 63:1). St. Augustine prayed the eternal truth 1,600 years ago, "Thou hast made us for thyself, O Lord, and our hearts are restless until they find their rest in Thee."[6]

Paul himself goes on in the wisdom text to name the source of his soul's satisfaction. He tells the Philippians, "I can do all things through Christ who strengthens me" (Phil. 4:13). Now, that does not mean Paul can grow tomato plants on the moon or win the lottery every week. It means Paul can be content whether he is in prison or a palace, in poverty or in prosperity. The outward circumstances do not paralyze the inward contentment. The secret of Paul's contentment was that his life was no longer at the mercy of external conditions. His deepest needs were all fulfilled in a relationship with God through Jesus the Christ. That friendship blessed Paul with power and peace, strength and salvation, comfort, and contentment.

Deep down we all have a need to connect with the Ground of our being, the Creator of the universe, the One in whom we live, move, and have our being. We need a source of hope, mercy, and grace. It is not a plan we need, but a person, a God with a face. We find the one in Jesus alone who provides that holy contentment that the world can neither give nor take away.

Mick Jagger has been singing for 55 years, "I can't get no satisfaction, I can't get no satisfaction, 'cause I try, and I try,

6 https://www.goodreads.com/quotes/42572-thou-hast-made-us-for-thyself-o-lord-and-our. Accessed September 9, 2020.

and I try, and I try...." Our soul satisfaction is not something we achieve by trying this or trying that. It is a gift we receive when we connect with Christ. When we accept that liberating gift, we can say with Paul, "If we have food and clothing, we will be content with these...."

In which tent will we choose to live? That of contentment or discontentment? Can we genuinely say with Paul, "I have learned to be content with whatever I have"? Benjamin Franklin cut to the chase in his observation, "Contentment makes poor men rich. Discontentment makes rich men poor."

Reflection Questions:

On a scale of 1-10, with 10 being absolutely content and 1 being totally discontented, where do you place yourself on most days?

What contributes to your discontentment?

What contributes to your contentment?

What insights did you gain from the four keys from Adam Hamilton?

Which key is the most helpful on a given day? Why?

CHAPTER FIFTEEN

Jesus in a Pandemic World

Wisdom Text: Isaiah 41:10

The planet has a problem. While an outbreak of a viral pandemic disease is daily taking hundreds of human lives across the world, we are also experiencing an outbreak of fear. The global health challenge is reported daily with almost always increasing figures of Covid-19 diagnoses, dangers, and deaths. The fear is as viral as the infection itself. By spring of 2021, already over 400,000 U.S. citizens have died from the virus. More than 2 million persons worldwide have lost their lives.

A national news article in late June 2020 had this deadline, "The next pandemic crisis could be a wave of suicides." Losses of jobs, income, and hope all contribute to a grim prediction that as many as an additional 75,000 persons could die from "deaths of despair" fearing the wave of the coronavirus epidemic. The number of cases across the U.S., the United Kingdom, Mexico, Russia, South Korea, Brazil, and other nations has exceeded 28 million men and women, the aged, children, and all in between.

Front-line workers, PPE, HHS, CDC, FDA, WHO, social distancing, and sheltering in place have entered our vocabulary on a too frequent basis. Education, worship, and work have gone virtual. Zoom has zoomed. Sports have disappeared for a season or more. No Final Four College

Basketball Championship. No sacred Masters Golf Tournament. No Major League Baseball Spring Training.

Fear is real and rampant in this season in our nation and world. People of color, folks without work, and those chronologically-gifted are especially vulnerable. The unseen virus has raised anxiety everywhere. The impact of lost jobs on small businesses, large industries, and the lives of families is staggering. Anxiety is high in the nation as there is political sparring, petty partisan politics, government grifters, racial tensions, and contentious national elections. Certainly, some fear is healthy in our lives which leads us to respect speed limits, rattlesnakes, and the Internal Revenue Service.

Choosing Faith Over Fear

In the first prehistoric stories of the Hebrew-Christian narratives, the first man (*Adam* in Hebrew) and the first woman (*Eve* in Hebrew means "life" represent all of humankind. They were made for each other. The tale tells us the two were taken in and shaken down by a shifty serpent. The Creator called to the creatures, "Where are you?" Adam answered, "I heard the sound of you in the garden, and I was afraid...and I hid myself." Fear led to the first sin in the scripture, lying to God.

Fear has been around since Day One. The tale of Adam and Eve is the story of humankind. We are anxious and afraid. Where do we turn to find strength and help in time of need? The planet has been there before. Survivors of World Wars I and II trooped forward in fearful times. Our nation was encouraged in 1933 by a paralyzed President who proclaimed in his inaugural speech, "We have nothing to fear but fear itself." Pandemics, wars, and stock market crashes have come and stayed for a season. The Hundred Years War lasted 116 years from 1337-1453. It was an intermittent battle between English and French rival dynasties. The present pandemic has its own battle fatigue as it expands in diagnoses, compassion fatigue, and deaths.

There is another option in the battle with ever-present fear. The Judeo-Christian tradition offers faith as a time-tested foundation in a pandemic world. When pandemonium strikes in a pandemic, the gift of faith is always available to all who will choose it. Fear is real. Faith is real. Faith has the power to trump fear.

Three Sources of Faith

Choosing faith over fear is the launching pad, whatever your past or present faith orientation or experience. Whether you have been christened, baptized, confirmed, or ordained, what matters is being grounded in faith. In a world which is sometimes upside down, downside up, or even sideways, there are three alliterative sources for strengthening your faith.

Source #1: The Scriptures of Faith

The Bible is a storybook, a history book, a worship book, a law book, a book of letters, a prophetic book, and, above all, a source of faith. The Bible is a library of 66 books. Faith beats in the hearts of the various books. When it comes to faith and fear, both are frequently mentioned. These proclamations from various biblical texts leave no ambiguity regarding the central role of faith in a pandemic world of much fear. There are five promises of providential presence, protection, assurance, and victory in a single verse:

Do not fear, for I am with you, do not be afraid,
for I am your God;

I will strengthen you, I will help you, I will uphold you with my victorious right hand.

Psalm 41:10

Other scriptures pregnant with providential promises regarding faith and fear:

Thus says the Lord: 'Do not be afraid because of the words you have heard.

Isaiah 37:6

Be a rock and refuge for me, a strong refuge to save me.

Psalm 31:2

Even though I walk through the darkest valley, I fear no evil; for you are with me.

Psalm 23:4

Lead me to the rock that is higher than I; for you are my refuge, a strong tower against the pandemic.

Psalm 61:2-3

Fear not. Listen, I bring you good news of great joy for all the people. A Savior is born. Peace on earth.

Luke 2:10-14

There is no fear in love, for complete love casts out fear.

I John 4:18

Do not be afraid, little flock, for it is your Father's good pleasure to give you the kingdom.

Luke 12:32

These Bible verses are but a handful of the many which call God's people to trump fear with faith. Tradition declares that the Good Book contains 365 versions of this essential command, "Do not be afraid." The true Commander-in Chief calls us every day of every year not to be afraid. We are the beloved children of God. Jesus loves us this we know, for the Bible tells us so.

Source #2: The Songs of Faith

Speaking of music, most Christian worship services are at least 50 percent music. Much of that is vocal. The traditional hymns and anthems, along with some more contemporary praise and worship, have much to teach us about faith in the face of fear. These titles and texts are representative of the plethora of faith-enhancing musical texts easily accessible in hymnals and songbooks.

Faith of fathers, living still, in spite of dungeon, fire, and sword,
O how our hearts beat high with joy whenever we hear that glorious word.
Faith of our fathers, holy faith. We will be true to thee till death.

How firm a foundation, ye saints of the Lord,
Is laid for your faith in his excellent word.
What more can he say to you than to you he hath said,
To you who for refuge to Jesus have fled?

In our end is our beginning, in our time infinity,
In our doubt there is believing, in our life eternity.
In our death, a resurrection, at the last a victory,
Unrevealed until its season, something God alone can see.

Be still, my soul, your God will undertake
To guide the future, as in ages past.
Your hope, your confidence let nothing shake,
All now mysterious shall be bright at last.

Source #3: The Service of Faith

"Serve the Lord with gladness" is a central call in the Hebrew-Christian scriptures. Serving is not optional according to Psalm 100:2. In the Gospels of Matthew and Luke, Jesus says, "The greatest among you is the one who serves." Jesus washed the feet of his disciples in a profound act of service on final evening with them. Servants in a faith community teach children, guide youth, sing in choirs, go on mission trips, invest in eternity with tithes and offerings, dust, paint, wash dishes, and serve on leadership teams.

Many folks of all ages, places, and means have heard this sweet whisper along life's journey, "Well done, good and faithful servant. Enter into the joy of your Master." It is normally a genuine joy to serve others. There is an intrinsic spiritual reward to those who serve. For faith folks, serving comes with God's package.

During the 2020/2021 pandemic and other times of crisis, we have seen saints in masks and other PPE step up and step out to save many lives. Their moral compass, often grounded in faith, has called them to serve and save others at the risk of their own lives. Their service casts out fear and replace it with trust in Jesus the Christ, the Holy One of God.

The 2020/2021 pandemic is not the first to be met by people of faith in fear's face. In 1793, a mysterious deadly disease emptied the streets of Philadelphia. The young nation's capital and largest city was being ravaged by yellow fever. On a considerably smaller scale, the epidemic presented challenges similar to the COVID-19 pandemic. Just as now, people of faith have stood up and stood out in responding in faith rather in fear.

Two African-American Methodist front-line heroes stepped up. Their names were Richard Allen and Absalom Jones. Jones wrote, "It was our duty to do all the good we could to our suffering fellow mortals." These men of faith were living "true to their Methodist convictions," recounts historian Anna Louise Bates in the April 2020 issue of *Methodist History.* She shares how the pair of pastors responded to the yellow fever outbreak in the City of Brotherly Love in the late 18th century. In August 1793, the virus infected thousands in the premier port city. Fear and financial hardship ensued. Over 20,000 citizens fled, frightened for their lives, including President George Washington and Secretary of State Thomas Jefferson.

The government of the new nation essentially ground to a halt. Most citizens sheltered in place, especially the non-affluent. Dr. Benjamin Rush, a prominent medical doctor, and signer of the Declaration of Independence, declared an epidemic in the city. The physician called on Allen and Jones for assistance. Both born in slavery, became pastors, and gained respect in the Brotherly Love City.

The Methodist connection to confronting yellow fever

pandemic extended beyond the scriptures, songs, and service 18th century. U.S. Army General Walter Reed confirmed mosquitos as the source of the disease. General Reed's father was a Methodist minister.

None of us is likely to have a hospital named after us. Yet, all of our names are in *The Lamb's Book of Life.* The scriptures, songs, and service we share in the name and for the sake of Jesus Christ our Lord trump faith over fear today, tomorrow, and forever. Thanks be to God!

Reflection Questions:

What is an area of your life where choosing faith over fear would make an immediate impact?

When you read, "all of our names are in the Lamb's Book of Life," how did that make you feel?

CHAPTER SIXTEEN

Jesus and 4-G Thanksgiving

Wisdom Text: Psalm 100

The fourth Thursday of November is Thanksgiving Day. This tradition of a national day of thanksgiving was established by President Abraham Lincoln on October 3, 1863 in the middle of a most uncivil Civil War. In 1941, the U.S. Congress established the fourth Thursday as Thanksgiving Day in our nation. What does Thanksgiving mean to you? What are you giving thanks for each Thanksgiving Day and each day?

In November 2016, Duane Gryder shared a list of things for which he is thankful. The first item was particularly timely:

> ***I am thankful that we only elect presidents once every four years.***
>
> ***I am thankful I am not a turkey this month.***
>
> ***I am thankful that hugs and kisses do not add weight or cause cancer.***
>
> ***I am grateful that teenagers will grow up and that one they will have children who will become teenagers of their own.***
>
> ***I am thankful that God's love never fails.***

Whatever you are grateful for each Thanksgiving, it is good, as the author of Psalm 92 begins her song of praise, "to give thanks to the Lord." This familiar wisdom text of Psalm 100 lifts four key components of worshiping God. They all begin the letter "G" and come directly from the text.

G #1 is Gladness

The text commands, "Worship the Lord with gladness. Come into his presence with singing." The dominant emotion of worship is gladness, not sadness. The dominant expression of worship is singing with joy, not sighing with sorrow. The authors of other psalms declare, "I was glad when they said to me, 'Let us go into the house of the Lord.'" "I will sing of loyalty and justice to you, O Lord. I will sing."

God's people rejoice, sing, and are glad to be in God's house together because they worship with gladness – the up and in, the down and out, and all in between are welcome. Have you heard of a movement crossing our nation of people wearing a safety pin on their lapel? The unobtrusive pin is an invitation to conversation with and for folks who are feeling fearful or uncertain because of racial, health, economic, or political concerns.

However we are processing the present national and international political landscape, we are glad to have a safe place to be welcomed to worship the Lord with gladness, hope, and caring in a hospitable community. Sanctuaries are safe places of glad inclusion, not sad exclusion.

G #2 is Gratitude

Especially in late November we express a profound sense of gratefulness – for who God is. The psalm reminds us, "Know that the Lord is God. It is he that made us, and we are his; we are his people, the sheep of his pasture." Some Sunday in worship turn to your neighbor and say, "Neighbor, God made you…you are his creation…you are his sheep."

Every time we celebrate a baptism, we are reminded that God has named us and claimed us. We are thankful that in our living and in our dying, we belong to God. We are grateful that whether we are in Colorado or Texas or California or New York or Alabama or Tennessee or Virginia some other state or nation, we belong to God's family.

We enter God's presence each day in gratitude. It is good, indeed, to give thanks to the Lord. We are thankful in this land for freedom, for the rights to vote, to assemble and to protest, and to worship.

In my last and longest pastorate of twelve years, members of the church's Board of Trustees sent personal handwritten letters to members of the large congregation. Inside was a kind note from the Trinity Church leaders thanking each donor for gifts to the church for a recent building renewal campaign. These nice volunteers took hours and hours, days, and days, to write hundreds of thank-you notes to everyone who gave over-and-above gifts.

The Trustees of the church did it all for one reason: to express gratitude, to say thanks for the amazing generosity of the church family one more time. Psalm 100 summons the people of God, "Enter God's gates with thanksgiving... Give thanks to him." Ongoing gratitude is part of our 4-G Thanksgiving. Every church pastor, finance committee, and board of trustees is grateful for the generosity of its members.

G #3 is Goodness

Look at verse five of the text. The Psalmist says simply, "For the Lord is good." What a gentle, yet crucial core theological affirmation. Sometimes folks default into unhealthy, misunderstandings of the nature of God. They perceive the Divine as primarily vengeful, angry, destructive, and out to get us. Those perceptions are mistaken. The text tells us in no uncertain terms, "For the Lord is good; his steadfast love endures forever." For the Lord is what? GOOD. God's LOVE, steadfast love, endures for how long? FOREVER. God is good. We are truly thankful for God's goodness, compassion, mercy, and grace. We declare that we are here for good. We say and pray, "Surely goodness and mercy shall follow me all of the days of my life."

G #4 is Generations

The writer concludes this psalm of thanksgiving with this magnificent affirmation of the Holy One: "God's steadfast love endures forever, and his faithfulness to all generations." In other words, no one is excluded by time or place from God's love.

Each year in November, the Roman Catholic Church, the Anglican Communion, and most Protestant churches celebrate All Saints Sunday. The service remembers those members and loved ones and friends who have joined the Church Eternal in the past year. Many congregations print and read the names of the members who graduated to glory in the past since All Saints Day. Then everyone in the congregation has the opportunity to honor the lives and memories of their extended family and friends who had departed this world in the last twelve months.

In January 2016, my mother-in-law died at age 90. In November 2016, my wife was in Texas to welcome our first granddaughter to this world – all five pounds and five ounces. Thanks be to God for Annie. Though great-grandmother did not get to greet great-granddaughter in this life, the good news of Psalm 100 is that "God's steadfast love endures forever, and God's faithfulness is to all generations." All generations.

We give great gratitude that God's grace is given across, through, and beyond "ALL GENERATIONS". The Bible declares, "A generation yet unborn shall praise the Lord." ALL generations belong to God. 4-G Thanksgiving – Gladness, Gratitude, Goodness, and Generations.

When British author Rudyard Kipling was at the height of his popularity, it was often said that every word Kipling wrote was worth 25 shillings. A group of Oxford students, tongue in cheek, wrote Mr. Kipling a letter. "Dear Mr. Kipling. Enclosed find 25 shillings. Please send us your best word." A few days later a telegram came back. It bore a single-word response – "Thanks." "Thanks" is a powerful word. Giving thanks is a good thing to do with gladness, gratitude, goodness, and by all generations.

Dick Enberg retired in 2016 year from a career of almost 60 years as a sports broadcaster. He broadcasted for many years for NBC, CBS, and ESPN. His voice was known around the nation and beyond as he covered Super Bowls, World Series, Wimbledon Tennis, and The Masters Golf Championships. He was recently given the Sports Lifetime Achievement Award. It has been said of Dick Enberg, "He was always the right man for the right moment."

Recipient of a Ph.D. in health sciences from the University of Indiana many years before, Dick Enberg was asked to be the speaker at the school's graduation several years ago. This is what he said to the 20,000 students, faculty, and guests:

"There are two words that express kindness better than any other: Those two words are 'Thank you.'

"By using these words in my 40 years of work I have never had one person refuse to accept them or fail to respond positively."

Paul wrote, "Be kind to one another…Rejoice always…Pray without ceasing and in everything give thanks for this is the will of God in Christ Jesus for you."

Good, gracious, and generous God, we thank you with and for the 4 G's: Gladness, Gratitude, Goodness, and Generations. For it is your will and our desire to be thankful people. In your holy name, we pray. Amen.

Reflection Questions:

Which "G" word comes easiest for you?

Which is least easy?

When did Jesus give thanks? (See Mark 14:22-23, Matthew 11:1125-27, John 11:41-42, Luke 23:34)

What several things are you most grateful for?

How did Jesus model giving thanks?

CHAPTER SEVENTEEN

Jesus and Pets

Wisdom Text: Psalm 36:5-9

Have you have ever had a pet in your family? A dog? Cat? Hamster? Fish? Bird? Horse? Turtle? Snake? Tarantula? Other animal? Almost 70 percent of American households have one or more pets. Pets play a major part in so many families and in our culture. Look under "P" in the Yellow Pages and you will find hundreds of pet businesses available in any metropolitan area - not just boarders, groomers, suppliers, and vet services, but also pet hospitals, day care centers, hotels, ranches, poop scoop services, crematories, and cemeteries.

Of course, the Internet is full of pets for sale: you can pick up a pure breed for $4,0000, and you can even find pet obituaries. The fact is, according to the American Pet Products Association, we spent over $95.7 billion in 2019 on our pets.[7] On top of all that, believe it or not, there are pet blogs and social media sites. You know, Facebook for Fido.

There are several special days and months connected to pets:

- January is Walk Your Pet Month.
- March 23 is National Puppy Day.
- April 11 is National Pet Day.

---

7 American Pet Products Association. "Pet Industry Market Size & Ownership Statistics" https://www.americanpetproducts.org/press_industrytrends.asp. Accessed August 20, 2020.

- Believe it or not, April 26 is National Hairball Awareness Day.
- There is a national Take Your Dog to Work Day each June.
- ...and on and on and on.

In October 2015, the *Denver Post* had this feature story: "Home Design with Pets in Mind." It shared how pet owners are "Most concerned with making it easier for their pets to eat, sleep, play, etc. on their own terms with as much independence as possible." On Valentine's Day, the paper printed an article entitled "Including Pets in Retirement Plans." What about the prominent place a plethora of pets play in our nation? We reflect on why pets play such a prominent role in our families and our culture, how they contribute positively to our lives, and what their role is in God's kingdom - past, present, and future.

We begin by recognizing and, indeed, celebrating that there is a special connection between people and their pets. Have you heard of the Denver Dumb Friends League? It was founded in 1910 and has helped over two million animals in the last 110 years. Its mission is "to end pet homelessness and animal suffering and to nurture the bond between pets & people."

What is this special bond between pets and people? It all has to do with things that are vital to our lives: friendship, companionship, and unconditional love. A veterinarian in my Denver congregation, Dr. Ji Rha, was gracious to share with me several insights in stories of people and their pets. She once cared for a greyhound named Bowser who died. The dog's owner wrote, "Dr. Ji. It's taken me some time to get over Bowser's passing. I don't want to sound too weird, but he taught me so much about life and love. I had somewhat of a crummy upbringing and a lot of things some people take for granted were missing in my life when I was growing up. Bowser showed me what unconditional love really meant and little did I realize just how much 'an animal,' would affect me so deeply. The book you gave me, *Every Dog an Angel,* really helped me take comfort in knowing there are many of us people out there who have incredibly special relationships with their pets." There are many folks who have such special relationships.

Dr. Rha wrote of her vet practice, "I am touched by the human-animal bond every day." She points out the roles of companionship animals play in families. Think of the holiday cards you receive which "Merry Christmas from Bob and Margie, Grant (15), Melissa (13), Jerry (11), and Fluffy the Cat or Bingo the Dog." So many pet owners, Dr. Rha notes, refer to their pets as their "partners, soul mates, or best friends."

Is it any wonder that dogs are brought into nursing, rehab, and other care centers where people are living with major health issues? The dogs have a therapeutic effect: lowering blood pressure, raising serotonin levels, and offering unconditional friendship and affection. There is a volunteer organization called PAWS (Pets Are Wonderful Support) whose mission is "Dedicated to preserving the human-animal bond." They provide animal companions to low income senior adults, disabled individuals, and persons with HIV/AIDS.

Stray shelter dogs are being been taken into correctional institutions where nonviolent prisoners care for them. The dog fostering program has turned into a unique rehabilitation process for the inmates who care for the dogs, encouraging them to find love, empathy, and faith within themselves.

Ask Siri for "Dogs on The Inside" to learn more about this mutually beneficial, life transforming partnership.

A connected lesson from pets: *We learn from them.* They make us better people. They teach us to love others. They connect with others regardless of age, race, gender, sexual orientation, religion, political preference, or income.

Pets make a positive difference in our lives. Susan is a member of our church. She owns a dog sitting service, so she is around a lot of canines. She was kind to share these lessons: "Some things I have learned from dogs:

- Be content with your surroundings.
- Enthusiastically greet each day.
- Live in the present.
- Trust your master.
- Love unconditionally.
- Exercise every day (a walk with your dogs does wonders for your spirit and your body).
- Age gracefully.
- Greet everyone like a new friend."

In her book *Bread of Angels,*[8] Barbara Brown Taylor writes, "A dog or cat can become a soul friend who knows how you are feeling when no one else does. I have a cat named Merlin who is my spiritual director. When I am frantic, he goes to sleep on my lap. When I am sad, he leaps out at me from dark corners...and when I am fine, he takes a break and goes off to do things on his own. Some people say we pick pets that look

8 Barbara Brown Taylor, *Bread of Angels,* Cowley Publications, 1997.

like us. If it is true, it is because they are really extensions of us, creatures who are so much a part of our lives that is it sometimes not easy to tell who belongs to whom."

Is it any wonder that we grieve when our precious pets - feline, canine, equine, and other line - die? We cry, we mourn, and we honor their memories. Someone shared with me a brochure from the Pet Loss Support Group which meets weekly in Denver. You can find it online – PetLossDenver.org

Several times in the past fifteen years persons of strong faith and deep commitment have asked sincerely and seriously after their pet died, "Do you think my dog is in heaven? Do you think I will see my pet again?"

How would you have answered those questions? The frequency and passion of the questions drove me to begin to reflect on a theology of animals in general and pets in particular, something I had not seriously ever done.

I began to look at the Bible and Christian tradition to see some things I had not paid much attention to. From the prehistoric narrative of Genesis, we witness these theological truths:

- God created the animals from the same ground that the first human is created.
- Animals and humans are kin and partners.
- The first human names the animals, like children, as a part of a living family in the Garden of Eden.
- God makes a covenant with Noah to never destroy the world with a flood. That everlasting covenant, symbolized by a rainbow, is with all flesh, including domestic animals (Genesis 9:10).

- The Psalmist summons all creatures, including animals, to praise the Lord, as we have sung (Psalm 148).
- The prophet Isaiah's vision of the peaceful kingdom is one in which all of the animals of the earth shall get along and a little child shall lead them (Isaiah 11:6-9).
- The vision of heaven in Revelation 5 is one of 24-7 praise to the Lamb of God by all of the living creatures in heaven and on earth and under the earth and in the sea.
- Significant segments of the Christian community have long held annual blessings of the pets and animals services. (By the way, that is best done in a park or other green spaces, and not in a sanctuary.)

In his 1998 book, *On God and Dogs: A Christian Theology of Compassion for Animals,*[9] Professor Stephen Webb notes, "The Bible treats animals as others who are really different and yet similar enough to merit kindness and to be included in God's plan for the world."

Perhaps, you are thinking I am equating pets with people. I am not. Pets will never lie, cheat, steal, or gossip.

Certainly, cats and dogs are the most common human pets. And they are different animals. A dog says, "You pet me, you feed me, you shelter me, you love me, you must be God." A cat says, "You pet me, you feed me, you shelter me, you love me, I must be God."

By the way, in a recent Gallup Poll, 68 percent of the respondents said they gave their pets a gift at Christmas. On a more significant level, another poll showed that 57 percent

---

9 Stephen Webb, *On God and Dogs: A Christian Theology of Compassion for Animals,* Oxford University Press, 1998.

of Americans said scientists should not do research in which animals would experience pain and suffering.

But back to the question, do dogs and other pets go to heaven?

American humorist Will Rogers said, "If there are no dogs in Heaven, then, when I die, I want to go where they went."

Again the words of the wisdom text, Psalm 36: "Your steadfast love, O Lord, extends to the heavens ... You save humans and animals alike, O Lord." The original Hebrew word there for "save" is "yasha," meaning "to be liberated, preserved, given victory to."

On March 7, 2016, Trinity member Dr. Ned Brainard wrote this tribute to a beloved, loyal pet. Perhaps you can identify with his experience of loss and love which outlasts this world:

Today, a good dog passed away. We said goodbye this day to Roo – A Good Dog.... Roo followed us everywhere we went. If we were in the Living Room, he was there. The Family Room, Roo was there. In his earlier years four paws would follow us upstairs. As he aged in recent times, Roo needed to be carried. If we went upstairs without him, Roo would wait faithfully in the Front Hall for our return. As the years took their toll, he never complained. He accepted his life as it was – always a loyal friend, always a picture of unconditional love.

As we remember Roo, two writings come to mind. One is the children's book, All Dogs Go to Heaven. Another is Nobel Prize Winner Rudyard Kipling's poem, A Dog for Jesus. It is about the loss of his dog. A portion of the poem includes this personal picture:

I wish someone had given Jesus a dog. As loyal and loving as mine.
To sleep by His manger and gaze in His eyes and adore Him for being divine.

As our Lord grew to manhood His faithful dog, Would have followed Him all through the day....

Well, the Lord has a dog now, I just sent Him mine, The old pal so dear to me.

And I smile through my tears on this first day alone, Knowing they are in eternity.

Day after day, the whole day through, Wherever the road inclined

Four feet said, "Wait, I'm coming with you." And trotted along behind.

Dr. Brainard concluded his note with these words, "And so today we said goodbye to Roo, our faithful friend – A Good Dog. Roo will remember us. We will so often remember our loyal dog. Our hearts are broken, but for Roo we wish many a romp in grassy fields and perhaps a squirrel to chase."

We certainly grieve the losses of our beloved pets. Do you think our pets grieve when we die? In 2011 Trinity member Johnny Merrill was hiking a Fourteener – El Diente Peak in the San Juan Mountains of Southwest Colorado. The 30-year-old political consultant was hiking with his dog Oof on the mountain's south face. Johnny had reached 13,500 feet when rocks began to fall. He had just called his pregnant wife to tell her he was about an hour from the summit.

No one knows exactly what happened, but Johnny was killed by the rockslide. What the recovery team does know for sure is that Oof, Johnny's Alaskan malamute mix who survived the slide, refused to leave his master's body through the dark, cold night. Oof was truly doggedly devoted to his deceased friend.

Friends, may we somehow, someway be somewhat worthy of the love and loyalty we receive from our pets. Perhaps their devotion reflects the Divine Creator who loves and saves all two and four-legged creatures alike.

Holy God, Lord Jesus of heaven and earth and all created things, including precious pets: Give us such faith, that we may commit ourselves and those precious us to us to your never-failing, steadfast, heavenly love for eternity. Thank you saving humans and animals alike. In your awesome grace through the Lamb of God, the Lion of the tribe of Judah, we pray, and someday die. Amen.

Reflection Questions:

What pets did you have as a child?

Can you remember their names?

Which was your favorite and why?

Do you have a pet now? If so, what role does she or he play in your family?

What lessons did you gain from this wisdom tale?

CHAPTER EIGHTEEN

Jesus and My Life Purpose

Wisdom Text: Micah 6:1-8

What is my purpose in life? Why am I here? How can my life make a difference? How can I find meaning in my life? How can I discover God's purpose for me? Ever ask any of those questions? In 2002, a California pastor named Rick Warren wrote a book called *The Purpose-Driven Life.* It sold 30 million copies. In 2004, approximately 1,200 people studied the book in small groups in the Texas church I was serving at the time.

Without a purpose, our lives can soon become a meaningless round of activities with self-preservation as the top priority. Indeed, sometimes survival is our goal: hanging in there until the weekend, payday, summer, the kids are raised, the mortgage is paid, or until retirement. These are interim goals – some short, some long – which motivate us and give us some sense of purpose.

But do we have a larger purpose in life than that? It is a good question on the first Sunday of the new year. If someone asks us when we were born, we could all answer that question. But what if someone asks, WHY were we born? The answer to that question is not on our birth certificates. An alarm clock can tell us when to get up in the morning; but what it cannot tell us is WHY? Why should we get up?

The question is: Why were we born? What is our purpose in life? The biblical witness is that we are to experience full, meaningful, and abundant lives – lives which fulfill God's intention for us. How do we fulfill our God-given purpose? We were born to live fully in response to the Holy One. We discover that purposeful and full life as we fulfill three expectations that God has for us. These three expectations come to us from the First Testament prophet Micah. In our reading for today, Micah recounts all God has done for his people from the time of the Exodus until the present – that is the eighth century B.C.E. – how many times and in how many ways God had acted to save them.

What was to be their proper response to God's saving acts? Are they to bring burnt offerings in worship? Are they to give countless animals and crops? Does God want their first-born children as a sacrifice for sin?

"No!" cried Micah. None of these. "God has shown you what is good." God has revealed your purpose in life, your proper response to his salvation. If you want to follow God's plan, if you want to live a truly fulfilling life, God requires three things of you: 1) Do justice; 2) Love kindness; and 3) Walk humbly with your God.

These three short, simple commands – a summary of the legal, ethical, and spiritual requirements of religion – are the keys to discovering meaning and purpose in one's life.

We were created to do these three things:

Thing 1: Do Justice

Several years ago, I was summoned to appear in a court of the justice of the peace, not as a defendant, but as a prospective juror. There were two crimes to be tried that day. Two citizens were accused of violating the law: one of going

42 MPH in a 30 MPH zone, and the other going 65 in a 55 MPH zone. I was not chosen for either jury panel, but the very next day I did receive a letter from the judge thanking me for my willingness to serve and reminding me that "trial by jury is the very cornerstone of our system of justice." The judge also shared with me the exciting news that in three weeks I would receive a check for $6.00 for having shown up in his court.

"Do justice," God says. God does not say, "Obstruct justice, or circumvent justice, or dispense with justice." *Doing* justice means more than adjudicating speeding tickets. It means an active concern for what is right, reasonable, fair, and truthful. It is rooted in the basic biblical concern for others – the hurting, the hungry, the homeless – and is based on the realization that we are our brother's keeper.

In his book, *Doing Justice in a Purple Congregation,* Dr. Jim Ryan shares a story of Mother Teresa. The tireless servant of the poor was once asked, "Why do you do what you do?" She answered, "I am a friend of Jesus. This is how I choose to live out that friendship." As friends and followers of the Son of God, our doing justice is a spiritual act of commitment. It is rooted in our relationship with Jesus. Our concern for justice leads us to rejoice that the minimum wage in the state of Colorado went up recently to $12.10 an hour. And, as of January 1, Colorado requires health care providers to disclose prices to the public. Colorado is doing justice.

Justice seeks change. Doing justice means we build Habitat for Humanity homes. Doing justice means we pray for peace. Doing justice may mean for some sharing in the Women's March this month or signing on the #Me, Too movement. Like Jesus, we have a concern for the abused, misused and falsely accused, for the poor, those who are denied fair treatment, those who need not only a handout, but a hand up in this rich nation to which we pledge "liberty and justice for all." There is sometimes a price to be paid for doing justice. We may be persecuted for righteousness sake, Jesus warns. But there is also a reward. And the reward is in discovering the fulfillment God calls us to in his gift of salvation in Christ our Lord.

Thing 2: Discover that meaning and purpose is through loving kindness.

Kindness is not a word you hear much, is it? You do not see it on the list of desired qualities of those who lead our state and nation, coach our professional teams, or lead businesses. However, we do rejoice in the generous compassion, concern, and caring expressed in multiple ways when tragedies happen. Strangers give blood. Gifts of prayers abound. Flowers, balloons, and memorials are tangible expressions of kindness and caring.

Several years ago, Joan Phillips gave a lovely answer to the question, "Why is congregational care important to you?" in an article in the Trinity Vision introducing the new chair of our Congregational Care Ministry. The Stephen Minister and grandmother replied, "Everyone has a story of a kindness that was extended to them, whether it's a hopeful word or a smile from a stranger or someone picking you up when you've become a 'puddle on the floor.' I know and appreciate the value of this gift of kindness."

I shared a message on mercy several years ago. "Loving kindness" is one translation of the Hebrew word for mercy. The New Testament continues the call of a loving, caring, sympathetic relationship with others through loving kindness:

- Jesus said, "Do unto others as you would have them do unto you" (Matthew 7:12).
- Jesus said, "Love one another as I have loved you" (John 13:34).
- Jesus said, "Love your neighbor as yourself" (Mark 12:31).
- Paul urged the followers of Jesus, "Be kind to one another, forgiving one another …."
- The fruit of the Spirit is … kindness and gentleness" (Ephesians 4:32).

In 1994, a Des Moines, IA synagogue was defaced with Nazi symbols painted on its outside walls. Leaders in the Christian community gathered on a Sunday afternoon at the synagogue to stand in solidarity with the Jewish congregation in reclaiming the space as holy ground. The senior pastor of the largest church in Iowa, an Assembly of God congregation, attended even though he knew he would catch holy heck from some in his congregation and from his evangelical colleagues.

As he stood in front of that large assembly of Jews and mainline Christians, he said, "We have become, in our society, way too good at giving each other a piece of our mind. Today I come to give you a piece of my heart." Giving others not a piece of our mind, but a piece of our heart, acting kindly and not harshly toward others is fulfilling God's plan and holy purpose for our lives in response to his saving kindness toward us in Christ Jesus.

Thing 3: Walking Humbly With Our God.

Walking is an action verb. It implies forward progress, energy, and effort on our part. It is something we do in following the Son of God. It is walking away from our past as Peter, James, John, and Andrew literally did when Jesus called them to be his disciples. We cannot stay where we are when God calls. We follow, we grow, we change, we give, we receive, and we are transformed as we travel the journey of faith and discipleship. We discover new horizons. We live life on purpose and with conviction. Note that we walk "humbly." Micah's command suggests that our walk is not in an arrogant, pretentious, or superior manner, but in a simple, confident, trusting way.

We also note that we are walking with God. We may pray, "Lord, walk with me today," or sing, "And he walks with me and he talks with me." The command in Micah is for us to walk with God. And if we are walking with God, then God is in charge. God is in charge of our lives, our values, our priorities, and yes, our pocketbooks. It is when we try to live life on our terms that we tend to mess things up. We will never enjoy the abundant, joyful, and fulfilling life as long as we are at the center of our lives. Jesus expressed the paradox this way, "Whoever keeps his life will lose it; but whoever loses his life for my sake and for the sake of the gospel will find it" (Matthew 16:25).

Does God have a purpose for our lives? You bet your life God does. And that purpose is experienced in our positive response to those words from scripture found in a Christmas card I received recently from the Urban Servant Corps of Denver. The card did not reference the birth of Jesus, but contained this biblical question and answer, "What does the Lord require of you? To do justice, to love kindness and to walk humbly with your God" (Micah 6:8).

As we live in a time of tension, trouble, and turmoil in public service, healthcare, and virus containment, racially motivated crimes and attacks, and dealing with a legacy of institutional racism, may we rediscover our purpose. Our purpose is to be here for good by doing justice, loving kindness, and walking humbly with our God. Jesus taught us our purpose in four words, "Love God, love neighbor."

Reflection Questions:

Are you acquainted with The Purpose-Driven Life?

If so, what do you know about it?

How do you do justice, express loving kindness, and walk humbly with the Divine One?

What is the main thing you want your obituary, tombstone, or final toast to say?

I once heard an evangelist say, "My purpose in life is to get to get to heaven and take as many people as possible with me." What is your life purpose?

Grow Your Faith

with these books from Market Square

marketsquarebooks.com

Discipler
Phil Maynard & Eddie Pipkin

Hear It, See It, Risk It
Steve Cordle

A Christian Teenager's
Guide to Surviving High School
Ashley Conner

HOPE
An Advent Journey
Olu Brown